100 Years

of Port Talbot Harriers

_1921 - 2021_

John Davies

In time-honoured alphabetical order, I am deeply indebted to the following people for helping me compile this history – Karl Angell, Colin Anthony, Gareth Ayres, Kevin Corcoran, Alan and Brenda Currie, Gareth Davies, Steve Davies, Frances Gill, Darren Grace, Leah Hayes and all the staff at Aberafan library, Bernie Henderson, Tony Holling, Chris John, Vince Lewis, Geraint Morgan, Mandy Morris, Derek Moss, Gaynor Oak, Jim O'Brien, Damian Owen, Alan Perkins, Andrew & John Phillips, Clare Phillips, Mario Rabaiotti, Paul Rees, Dillwyn Robbins and Christine Robbins (who loaned me Dil's diaries), Ian Swanson, Darren Vaughan, Charles Walsh, Dave Waters, Alex Williams

'Arthur'

We all know that athletics is all about athletes, but without officials there would not be any athletics. One of those great stalwarts, who literally gave his life to Welsh athletics, Arthur E. Williams, died after a short illness on 2nd November, 1983, aged 90.

Pen Portrait – Arthur E. Williams, MM, MBE 1893 – 1983
Port Talbot YMCA & Port Talbot Harriers

Arthur E. Williams had a record very few could equal. He served his club in one capacity or another for over 60 years. He was one of the founder members of Port Talbot YMCA Harriers (now Port Talbot Harriers) in 1921 and was still an active committee member in his capacity as president at the time of his death at the grand age of 90 in 1983.

He had been involved with all of the major developments in Welsh athletics and was president of the Welsh AAA for 17 years between 1959 and 1976.

At the time of his death, he was busily arranging for funds to be raised for the Los Angeles Olympics in his capacity as chairman of the Welsh branch of the British Olympic Association. Just three weeks earlier he had attended the Welsh AAA AGM at Brecon, taking his usual active part in the debates.

He was a familiar figure at all Welsh fixtures and was at home whether supervising the funnel at a cross country race or acting as a field referee at one of the major events at the White City. He officiated in the 1948 Olympic Games at Wembley. Although only slight in stature he had boundless energy and despite his advanced years he would drive his own car to athletics meetings, resplendent in his blazer and AAA badge.

He was also a regular contributor to Athletics Weekly as 'AEW' with his Welsh Notes and one of his reports appeared in the first ever issue on 7th January, 1950.

When the Welsh AAA instituted their 'Award of Honour' in 1952, Arthur was one of the eight initial recipients. In 1972, the AAA also awarded him the same honour. Before his death, he was due to attend the AAA's AGM at which he was to be re-elected as vice-president. He was also a Life Vice-President of the Welsh AAA.

He saw distinguished service in the Great War, during which he received the Military Medal in the field for bravery under enemy fire. A deeply religious man, he was a staunch Methodist and had been president of the Port Talbot Free Church Council. He was also holder of the Scouts Silver Cross for life saving. In 1964, he received the MBE for services to athletics.

Arthur, who was born in Bristol, moved to Port Talbot as a young man to work on the docks. A close friend of George Thomas, later Lord Tonypandy the former Speaker of the House of Commons who was born in Port Talbot, Arthur was a tireless worker for Welsh athletics in general and his contribution will certainly not be equaled for many decades to come – if ever.

This extract was taken from 'The History of Welsh Athletics' by kind permission of co-authors Alan and Brenda Currie – and what better way could you start a history of Port Talbot Harriers?

In fact, there would be no Port Talbot Harriers without Arthur Williams. Although there is little information on the very early days of the club, it is an established fact that Arthur, along with D.J.P. Richards founded the Port Talbot YMCA Harriers in 1921.

YMCA building in the background

1920s

Foundation - 1921

It's uncertain who the founding officials were, but Arthur Williams, David J. P. Richards (affectionately known as 'Dippy'), Will Owen and Rex Lewis were the only people known to be at that meeting held on 15th October, 1921. AEW became secretary in 1922 until 1944 and remained an active committee member all his life. Arthur's particular interest was cross country and he only retired from competing in his late 40s. As a Christian, it was only natural for him to turn to the YMCA when looking for a base for the Harriers. D.J.P. Richards was an outstanding athlete, and although joining Newport later, was winner of dozens of Welsh Championships.

Several newspaper reports have been found indicating that schools' athletics was thriving in the 1920s. It is pure speculation, of course, that this led AEW and DJPR to form the YMCA Harriers. At this time the YMCA building was an old shed opposite the Grand Hotel. Members of the Sea Rovers Troop of the Scouts attended and also joined the athletics section.

This was way before the digital age and times were manually recorded in fifths of a second *i.e.* 100 yards (not metres) won in 10 3/5 seconds. Another interesting fact is that there were very few running tracks in the country. Athletic events in Port Talbot were mainly held at the Talbot Athletic rugby ground on a grass track.

The first report found which mentioned a Port Talbot YMCA Harrier was dated 21/08/1922. D.J.P. Richards finished third in the one-mile race at the Welsh AAA Championships in Cardiff. Later in 1922, DJP won his first championship race. This was the Welsh Novices Cross Country Championship organized by PTYM and held in Margam Park.

In the 1923 Welsh T&F Championships, Will Owen sprinted to victory in the 100yards (10.2), beating Rowe Harding who was later to become captain of the Wales rugby team and a British Lion. Owen won the title again in 1924 (10.6).

In June 1927, 'a grand athletic sports (under AAA laws) took place at the Waverly Park, Clydach'. This was probably the first appearance of Isaac O'Brien who was later to become a prominent figure in British long-distance running. Ike, as he was known, took second place in both the 880 yards and the mile events.

Harry Anderson was a top-class sprinter and played for Aberavon RFC. He'd won the 220yards Welsh Champs while a member of Newport Harriers and went on to win the 100yds in 10.2 as a member of PTYM in 1929.

Athletics meetings in these early days included what some would regard as novelty events. Some of them would be for all age groups such as throwing the cricket ball, punting the football and obstacle race. Others for juniors included the sack race, 3-legged race, egg and spoon race. The most intriguing event has to be the flowerpot race! Held over 30-50 yards, the contestants had to stand on two upturned flower pots and use them as stepping stones. On the gun, they moved one pot forward, stood on it while they moved the second pot and so on until they reached the finish line. Anyone falling off had to return to the start.

Enough of the frivolity. The PTYMCA Harriers was a very successful team during the 1920s. The following extract was published in the South Wales Daily Post on 24th May, 1930:-

Although lacking in football and cricket teams, the Port Talbot YMCA possesses one of the finest Harriers clubs in Wales. In the annual YMCA reports, the Port Talbot team has never failed to perform conspicuously and has gained practically a monopoly in the competition for the Sir John Llewellyn Shield awarded to the institution with the biggest bag of points at the conclusion of the meeting. The record of the Port Talbot YMCA is indeed a noteworthy one. They were champions during the years 1922, 1923, 1925, 1926, 1928; runners-up in 1924 and 1927 and joint holders with Newport in 1929. Not only as a team has Port Talbot attained fame, but in D.J.P. Richards they have one of the finest athletes Wales has ever produced. He is the present four-mile champion of Wales, as well as having won in his career approximately fifty championships. Last year he was included in the British Isles team against France. The Welsh 220 yards champion is another member of the Port Talbot club and is Harry Anderson, an ex-Aberavon wing. I understand that Ronnie Boon, the Welsh international three-quarter, will assist the team this year.

Port Talbot YMCA Harriers Welsh YMCA champion side. Top row from left: Mr Albert Sheppard; G R Marshall; N Thomas; A E Williams (secretary); W Roberts; L Carpenter; D I Jenkins; G Kent. Front row: W R Watkins (general secretary); C J Williams; W Owens; F Pittard (captain); H J Anderson; D J P Richards; A Jenkins; Geo Harris (chairman).

1930s

At this time the majority of athletic events included only handicapped races. For example, over 100 yards the runner with the fastest season's best would start on scratch at 100 yards. The slower runners would be given a head start depending on their best times. The athlete with the slowest best would have, perhaps, only 90 yards to run. In theory, all the runners would cross the finish line at the same time (an official's nightmare!). In practice that rarely happened.

PTYM had a number of exceptional athletes. C.G. Cupid was a Welsh sprint champion (although he was only with PTYM for one season) and Arthur Foley excelled in the high jump. Jenkin White and John Thomas were acclaimed as the greatest exponents of the long jump and hop, step and jump (triple jump now). Isaac O'Brien was regarded as a promising distance runner.

Little is known about the early officers of the club, but Vincent Shipway was mentioned in 1930 as a former secretary. The incomparable AEW was beginning to make a name for himself as an organizer. The South Wales Daily Post carried this item about him on 13th June, 1930: -

Admired for his great sportsmanship and noted for his organizing capabilities, Mr. Arthur Williams, secretary of the Port Talbot YMCA Harriers, is doing noble work in preparation for the annual and most attractive sports of these institutions. Arthur, as the athletic world knows him, has done far more than his share in assisting Port Talbot's noted team of harriers to maintain their high standard of efficiency. He is recognized as a capable spotter of talent, and hardly a sporting event is held locally unless his advice is sought.

1931

In August 1931, Cupid proved unbeatable in a match against Swansea Valley, winning the 100 and 220 yards. Ike O'Brien also scored a double in the 880 yards and one mile, while Jenkin White won the long jump.

PTYM and Swansea Valley were reported as being the only clubs in West Wales who could cater for all branches of athletics. Later in the year, Cupid transferred to Swansea Valley. Harry Harber emerged as a new sprint prospect for PTYM.

1932

The YMCA championships were not held in 1932 because of a lack of challengers to Port Talbot's supremacy. The club was still going from strength to strength however. They were winners of many inter-club matches and several members won prizes in open sports events. Other prominent names were J. Williams winning an 880 yards race in 2 minutes 14 seconds and W. Collins taking first prize in a mile race in 5 minutes 04 seconds.

AEW made an interesting comment on fair play in one of his frequent newspaper articles: -

False starts come about by over-eagerness, but there is one aspect of the situation, in that it has a tinge of bad sportsmanship in trying to get away before the other competitors. It is no use quibbling, as on Saturday, at the starter because he recalled the runners. It was his duty to see that they had a perfectly fair start. I would like to give a tip. Sports promoters should see that the starter has a repeating pistol for recall purpose.

It soon became standard practice for starters to use repeating pistols.

Later in 1932, Harry Harber turned his hand to the 440 yards with remarkable success. In an inter-club match, he beat Welsh champion, Eric Hughes, recording an astounding time of 48$_{2/5}$ seconds.

Inter-works sports were very popular at this time. To promote this branch of athletics, Captain Leighton Davies JP, donated a trophy and was quoted as saying, 'Healthy rivalry on the sports field engenders good fellowship between all departments and develops esprit-de-corps within the works,'

1933

The 57$_{1/2}$-mile Newport to Swansea road relay held in February 1933 proved a disappointment for PTYM. They could only finish 13th out of fourteen teams in a time of 6 hours 17 minutes and 13 seconds, way behind winners Cwmbran who recorded a time of 5hrs 25-10.

PTYM seemed to be going through a fairly lean spell in 1933. In July, they could only manage 4th out of five in an inter-club sports held at St. Helen's, Swansea. It was not all doom and gloom though. Haydn Evans emerged as a promising sprinter, winning the 100 yards. Later in the year he placed 3rd in the 100 and won the 220 yards.

There was even better news from the Port Talbot Secondary Schools sports. Roy Williams, just 15 years old, notably achieved wins in seven different events. These were: - 100, 220, 440, 880, high jump, long jump and throwing the cricket ball. Roy also went on to win the high jump at the Ammanford Sports in July.

ROY WILLIAMS, of Port Talbot Y.M.C.A., winner of the high jump at Ammanford Carnival and Sports, goes over in fine style.

1934

In 1934, youngster Andrea Magdalino was selected for the senior West Wales team in the 220 yards. Other PTYM athletes selected were Harry Harber (440) and Cyril Evans (pole vault and high jump).

On July 19th, in a marathon race from the bottom of Stormy Down to St. Helen's, Swansea, W. Short of Newport was the winner in 2 hours 50 minutes. Ike O'Brien finished 4th in 3-26.

On August 9th, PTYM were reported as being the senior club in West Wales and making a pioneer visit to the newly formed Cwmavon Athletic Club.

The track season ended on a high note on 8th September at Hendy. Haydn Evans achieved 2nd place in the 100, 220 and shot. He also scored valuable points with 3rd in the discus to help PTYM win the West Wales Athletics League.

1935

In a league match in 1935, 'C. T. Evans put up a plucky show in the pole vault in which, while in mid-air in one of his early vaults, the pole, a brand new one, snapped in two, and he landed on his back from a height of six feet. Although severely shaken, he continued to jump and eventually won.'

In a match between West Wales and East Glamorgan, there were splendid performances from three PTYM athletes. Youngster, Fred Needs, won the javelin with a mighty throw of 136feet 6inches; Cyril Evans the pole vault with 8feet 71/4 inches, and B. H. T. Humphreys the shot with 31feet 9inches.

In May 1935, Llangenech entertained Neath YM and PTYM in a sports organized to raise funds for their newly formed club. At this event, Hubert Tossell, a newcomer to the PTYM team, vaulted superbly to claim victory over the expert Cyril Evans who had to be content with 2nd place.

In July, 1935, Andrea Magdalino was selected by the Welsh AAA to attend the coveted course in athletics at what was later to become Loughborough University. Magdalino was Victor Ludorum at the Aberystwyth University sports, winning the 100, 220, 440, 120 yards hurdles, high jump, 2nd long jump and 3rd in the shot.

The Evening Post of 27th July reported that plans had been prepared for a suggested asphalt cycle track around a 440-yard cinder running track at Vivian Park, Aberavon. The track was never built.

1936

There were no reports to be found for the early part of the year, but moving on to June, 1936, PTYM won an inter-club match at the Talbot Athletic ground. There were good wins for Cyril Evans in the pole vault and high jump and for Roy Williams in the 220 and long jump.

In July, PTYM went pioneering again to the Blaengwynfi Athletic club. The club had been the inspiration of PC Edgar Jones who proved his worth by beating his PT rivals in the discus, pole vault and long jump.

At the Llanelli Sports in August, 1936, Andrea Magdalino won the 100yds, high jump and set a new Welsh record in the javelin with a throw of 141feet 3inches (43.06 metres). At the same meeting Cyril Evans' pole (not the same one as before!) snapped again. He fell heavily, was badly injured and was unable to compete for the remainder of the season.

1937

February 26th, 1937 PTYM convened a meeting of Neath, Mansel Works, Cwmavon and Blaengwynfi in which the Mid Glamorgan Amateur Athletic League was formed for the development of amateur athletics.

The West Wales Championships were held at Morriston Park in August, 1937. Fred Needs set a new Welsh record in the javelin with 141feet 6$\frac{3}{4}$ inches. E. M. Jenkins won the shot, but the performance of the day was Jenkins' Welsh record of 116 feet 8$\frac{1}{2}$ inches in the discus, beating the previous record by a remarkable 18feet 8$\frac{1}{2}$ inches. It was a good year for PTYM athletes. Ike O'Brien won the Welsh Marathon and West Wales marathon; C. T. Evans won the Glamorgan, West Wales and Welsh pole vault championships. PTYM also won the inaugural Mid Glamorgan Athletic league. In the league match at Abergwynfi, Cyril Evans set a new Welsh record of 9ft 5ins for the pole vault.

In the summer of 1937, Ike O'Brien let it be known that he was in training to set up an official time for a 50-mile road run. During a series of 40-mile training runs, Ike was unaccompanied and had no means of sustenance. He did confess, though, that on one run a farmer had given him a glass of milk, and another time a scout had made him a cup of tea! Ike completed his run on 2nd October in 6hrs-20mins. He started from near Llangadock, then the route took him through Llandeilo – Carmarthen – Kidwelly – Llanelli – Forestfach to the finish at the Guildhall in Swansea. A feat of amazing endurance.

In October, PTYM runners Lyn Griffiths, Ike O'Brien and J. Roach claimed the first three places in a XC match with Swansea University held on Baglan Moors. PTYM won the match by 11 pts to 27 pts. Tom Winslade won the Junior Welsh XC Champs and was selected to represent Wales in the international match in Ireland.

The provision of playing fields with a combined cycle and running track was discussed at a meeting of the Borough Education Committee. Several sites in the borough were to be visited.

Training in the autumn had been geared to the highly regarded Newport to Swansea Relay Race. The course was 57½ miles and the team consisted of 11 runners, each running approximately 5 miles before touching the hand of the next runner in the relay. PTH finished in 5th place in what was nicknamed 'the longest game of touch in the world'!

The AGM was held in December, 1937. Officers elected were: - President – P. H. Burton, Chairman – H. Harber jnr, Secretary – AEW, Treasurer – C. A. Griffiths, Captain – C. T. Wright, Vice-Captain – B. Quick. The President's Cup for the best performance of the year was won by W. T. Williams.

1938

The first Annual Dinner of the Harriers at their YMCA headquarters on 15th January, 1938 proved a highly successful event. P. H. Burton, Chairman of the YMCA, presided and during the evening, trophies were presented to the winners of various events. These included framed photos to Ike O'Brien and Cyril Evans.

There was a huge turnout at the Talbot Athletic ground on Saturday 5th February, 1938 to take part in or watch a coaching demonstration by famous Finnish coach Armas Valste. Those present were not disappointed as he gave an effortless display of throwing the javelin, discus and putting the shot during which he easily beat all current Welsh records.

With Tom Winslade 8th and Brynley Quick in 9th place, PTYM excelled themselves at the senior Welsh XC Champs to record their best ever team position of 3rd. Tom was rewarded with a place in the Welsh team while Bryn was named as first reserve.

PORT TALBOT Y.M.C.A. RELAY TEAM at the West Wales Athletic championship at Kidwelly. Left to right: Roy Williams, Sydney Williams, C. D. Wright and R. Harber,

On April 8th, 1938, the first annual dinner of the Mid Glamorgan League was held at the Walnut Tree Hotel, Port Talbot. At this dinner, PTYM were presented with a 'handsome shield' given by Mr. D. M. Evans-Bevan JP as winners of the league the previous summer.

In May of 1938, PTYM won the first round of the Mid Glam League at the Talbot Athletic ground. The aptly-named B. Quick was a comfortable winner of the three-mile race.

In June, Ike finished 8th in the Polytechnic Marathon from Windsor to London in 2 hours 51 minutes 15 seconds.

In July, at the Mansel Works Sports, there were wins for Aberavon wing, Sid Williams, over 100 yards (10.2) and 220 yards (23.0). This seems to be the first local reporting of times to the nearest 0.1 second (instead of the previous fifths). There was also a win in the mile for club captain C. T. Wright in 4 minutes 32.0 seconds.

At the Welsh T&F Champs, there were gold medals for Lyn Griffiths in the 1 mile (4-52), Roy Williams 440yds (51.4) and Cyril Evans pole vault (10ft 2$_{1/2}$ins)

Despite wins for Cyril Evans (pole vault) and Fred Needs (javelin), PTYM had to concede victory to a strong Roath Harriers team in an exciting match which ended in semi-darkness at the Talbot Athletic ground. B. Quick was not quite quick enough, finishing second to Roath in both the 880 yards and mile races.

At the West Wales Championships in August, Ike O'Brien again won the marathon. *'He was in good form, which is surprising, for in a training run to Morriston from Port Talbot last week, he had 'misplaced a sinew in his foot'.* There were also wins for Welsh champion, Roy Williams in the 440yds, B. Humphreys in the shot and Fred Needs, showing his versatility, in the discus.

In the Pyle Sports, the improving Sid Williams recorded wins in the 100 (9.9) and 220 (22.3). Exciting young prospect, James Ll. Griffiths won the Welsh Junior one-mile championship in 4-52.

Even in the absence of Ike O'Brien PTYM scored a runaway victory in the 6th West Wales Inter-Club Champs for the Hendy Shield in a match at Kidwelly.

August 20th, 1938, Ike O'Brien ran the 50 miles from Cardiff civic centre to Swansea civic centre in 6 hours 27 minutes 42 seconds, accompanied by clubmate E. L. Carpenter. He carried a message from the mayor of Cardiff which he safely delivered to the mayor of Swansea. The letter expressed the Cardiff mayor's good wishes for the success of the YMCA sports. The week after his amazing achievement, this article appeared in print: -

In a little street in Aberavon, Ike O'Brien, the Welsh Marathon Champion, is having a terrible struggle against odds. He has been unemployed for over two years. Little did the people think when they applauded him on his run from Cardiff to Swansea last Saturday that he had to sell some of the trophies previously won to buy food for his wife and family, and to get that little bit of extra nourishment to help along the spirit of determination which is in him to bring fame to Wales. Ike O'Brien is looking for work every day. He is eager for it, but has met with nothing but disappointment. It is a human tragedy – one of many alas – 'but surely

Ike O'Brien 50-mile run, Cardiff to Swansea

something can be done in an industrial town like Port Talbot to give this big-hearted fellow some occupation', said one of his admirers. Discussing his triumphs on the road, Ike, who is 35, said marathon running has been his hobby for years and while he was in regular employment, he enjoyed it. But for the last two years it had been a struggle. People had been kind to him, he said, when he was taking part in big national events; and while in the throes of all the excitement he had created, there was the one black picture in the background – unemployment. Ike is a willing worker. He has been laboring in the tin works and on the dock, and is willing to tackle any job offered him.

Later in 1938, when offered a gift, Ike was heard to say that he didn't want charity. All he ever wanted was a job. Within a few weeks he was employed as an electrician's mate in the Guest Keen Baldwin Works at Margam.

At a meeting on the 19th October, it was revealed by YMCA chairman, P. H. Burton that sufficient funding had been received to make the dream come true of a new building to house the YMCA. The estimated cost was £8000. The National Fitness Council had awarded a grant of £4700, GuestKeenBaldwin had donated £1500 and promised a further £500. The Margam Estate provided the building site in Talbot Road at a peppercorn ground rent. It was anticipated that the building would be completed in a year's time.

The popular Newport to Swansea Relay Race held in November was won by Roath in 5-28-39. PTYM's time of 5-53-10 left them lying in 6th place.

Mr. T. E. Holdsworth of the National Fitness Council stated at a public meeting in December, 1938 that the PT Council had agreed in principle to the building of a cycle track. He added that cyclists primarily wanted a track for themselves, but this was not a reasonable proposition. It should be made into a cycling and running track with possibly a football field in the middle. AEW responded by saying by combining cycling with running the track should be a great success, as in Port Talbot they had one of the finest athletic clubs in Wales.

1939

On 14th January, 1939, PTYM were the winners of a road relay from Port Talbot YMCA to the Neath Conservative Club. That evening the club held their second annual dinner at the Grand Hotel where Ike O'Brien was awarded the P. H. Burton Cup for the outstanding performance of the year for his 2hrs 51-23 run in the Polytechnic Marathon.

In February, the building plans for the new YMCA headquarters on a site in Talbot Road were approved.

In early July, Ike recorded an improved time of 2 hours 47 minutes 33 seconds when finishing 5th in the British Marathon Championships. This was despite the recurrence of muscle trouble at 20 miles, probably caused by having to stand in the corridor nearly all the way to London in a crowded train. Later that month, he improved on that time in winning the Welsh Marathon Championship in a new record time of 2 hours 45 minutes. This was even more remarkable because of the poor weather and Ike also lost 2-3 minutes when he went off course!

The Port Talbot Hospital Carnival Committee organized a summer sports at the Talbot Athletic Ground where there was a high standard of competition. Fred Needs could only manage 3rd in the javelin where winner, A. R. Squibbs (Loughborough Uni) set a new Welsh record of 182 feet 10$_{1/2}$ inches (55.45 metres). D. J. P. Richards, still competing at the age of 42, won the two-mile walk by a huge margin, 'He walked away with it!'

The PTYM team was in a state of shock after finishing second behind Neath in the Mid Glam League at the Talbot Athletic Ground in August, 1939!

At the West Wales Championships in Kidwelly, Gwylim Treharne won the 100 and 220 yards sprints. Cyril Evans had a field day winning the pole vault, high jump, long jump and hop, step and jump.

In an article published on 1st September, 1939, the sports writer, Spikes, commented on the current state of political affairs: -

While we write these notes the crisis is at its most acute position, and by the time they appear in print, the worst may have happened, but we do feel that we must live up to the British tradition of carrying on our every day jobs while those in authority unravel the intricacies of the international mix-up. Again, if the worst should happen, we must be like Cincinnatus, who left his plough to help the state, or in other words, give up sport and play a part in civil defense.

Two days later, Britain declared war on Germany.

1940s

On the declaration of war, all championship and track & field events were cancelled. It seems there was nothing of an athletic nature to report in 1940.

There was an item of great news though. On 6th April, the new YMCA building was officially opened. A presentation key was used by Lady Wright, wife of well-known industrialist Sir Charles Wright, to open the door of the YMCA. This was followed by a dedication service held in the gymnasium and conducted by the Rt. Rev. Lord Bishop of Llandaff, John Morgan.

During the week following the opening of the new YMCA, a varied programme of activities took place. One of the more unusual events was a Bacon Flitch Trial. This was an ancient ritual the purpose of which was to award a flitch of bacon (half a pig) to a married couple who could satisfy the judge and jury that in *'a twelve month and a day they have not wisht themselves unmarried again'*. There was a close-fought contest between three couples, but winners of the flitch were Mr. and Mrs. W. D. Berry of Crown Street, Port Talbot.

In 1941, the only activity reported was a Home Guards sports meeting at Talbot Memorial Park on 23rd August. 'As the day turned out to be one more fitting for a swimming gala, the event was cancelled.'

The meeting took place the following Saturday and was a huge success. The organizing secretary was AEW, and there were open events in which Port Talbot's D. Parr won the 220 and was 2nd in the 100 yards. It was not simply serious athletics though. 'The satisfied crowd was treated to thrills and laughter' with such events as tug of war, bomb throwing, late for parade race (won by J. Poston) and the blind squad drill! A similar event was held at the Gnoll rugby ground by Neath ATC. Port Talbot ATC was second in the relay and, of course, AEW was officiating.

There were no athletic events reported in 1942, but Port Talbot schools were kindly lent the GKB ground for their annual event. In an open mile race, Ike was second to Ken Arnold. There were some familiar Port Talbot names like Mainwaring, Bamsey, Tobin and Harwood in the school sports.

There were no athletic events reported in 1943, but on 6th June, 1944, the YMCA of Britain celebrated its centenary. It was a double celebration because Port Talbot YMCA was celebrating its silver jubilee. In honour of the occasion, a service of remembrance was held and the doors of PTYMCA were thrown open to the general public to observe the members' various activities.

As part of the Civic Week a Sports was held at GKB, Margam in August 1943 where Sgt. Instructor Gold made a giant leap of 6ft0ins in the high jump. This was reckoned to be a Welsh record at the time

Later in June, the County School sports was reported in the Guardian. V. Wehrle was 2nd in the high jump and the three-legged race. (Wehrle & Sheehan were a notable firm of local solicitors). The winning house was Llewellyn, Tudor 2nd, Rhys 3rd and Glyndwr 4th.

After a lapse of twelve years, the YMCA Championship was held at the GKB, Margam ground, hosted by PTYM. A series of junior events were held because of the absence of so many senior athletes. Val Antolin was 2nd in the boy's 100 yards, but the highlight of the day was the debut of 15-year-old Albert O'Brien, who won the open mile and relegated his famous father, Ike into 3rd place. Team winners were Abertridwr Red Triangle Club. PTYM could only manage a disappointing 3rd place after dominating the event before the war.

1945

On January 13th, 1945, while engrossed in his work at GKB, Isaac O'Brien was severely injured by a moving crane. He survived for four weeks, but sadly died in hospital on the 11th February. The inquest returned a verdict of accidental death. How ironic that the job he had so eagerly sought should bring about the premature end of his illustrious athletic career and the end of his life.

An Appreciation by 'Spikes'

No matter what the weather, if you were out on the main road anywhere between Bridgend and Morriston, and hearing the patter of feet, turned your head quickly you would see a lean little fellow clad in shorts and vest trotting along the side of the road. You will see him no more, as there has passed on one of the greatest distance runners of modern times in the person of Isaac O'Brien, Port Talbot YMCA Harriers, Welsh Marathon Champion 1937/38/39. He was an athlete who brought credit to the sporting record of his club, town and country. He was known as a great-hearted athlete, who never talked about his prowess and was always ready to help novice runners. He was a model athlete and kept up his running to the end.

In July, 1945, several PTYM athletes were selected to represent West Wales. Sargent Len Madden was expected to do well in the sprints as was John Nash in the 3-mile race. Welsh Champion Cyril Evans was expected to have a comfortable victory in the pole vault. There are no results available but we are assured that there was a steady demand for tickets – Stand 1 shilling and 6 pence ($7_{1/2}$p); Field 1 shilling (5p); Children 6 pence ($2_{1/2}$p), and the Cwmafan Prize Band would be in attendance.

In August, PTYM harriers held a sports day at the Mansel Works cricket ground with the object of reviving interest in athletics after the war. There was a thrilling finish in the junior mile with a dead heat between 16-year-old Albert O'Brien (Ike's son) and a guest French athlete. Other PTYM winners were – Rita Evans (Girl's 80yds), Roy Bish (Youth's 100 & 220yds), G. Samuel (Open 100yds) and K. Arnold (Open 440yds and 1mile).

1946

The Welsh Youths Cross Country Championships were held in Cardiff in January, 1946. Albert O'Brien was the only entrant from PTYM and finished a creditable 4th. This was his first Welsh Championship race and it was a remarkable coincidence that his father Isaac ran in his first championship twenty-one years before and also finished 4th.

In February, 1946, a cross country match with Llanelly (this is how it was spelt then) County School Harriers was held on the Baglan Moors. After team captain, Idwal Hopkins, had laid out a paper trail, there was an intense tussle for the lead between V. Griffiths of Llanelly and O'Brien. Griffiths eventually proved the stronger with O'Brien a close second. Llanelly won the match. In his report, journalist, Spikes, added: - 'I have been asked to broadcast an appeal for spiked running shoes which may be lying on dusty shelves or in dark cupboards. Young athletes cannot get these and will buy any second-hand ones. Old sportsmen who are willing to part with them should let me know.' (My first pair of running spikes were hand-me-downs from my brother-in-law in 1967. The spikes were fixed into the front part of the sole – not screw-in as they later became.)

Also, in February, 1946, PTYM Harriers held its AGM. The chairman, Mr. George Butler, paid tribute to AEW for his twenty-one years' service as secretary. 'The Association was very proud of him, and life membership, the highest honour that the Association could give, was now being conferred.'

The 5-mile Mumbles road race was re-instated in April 1946. Albert O'Brien continued to show great promise finishing 8th against more experienced runners. In the same month, AEW was elected vice-president of the Welsh AAA.

On May 12th, 1946, a framed plaque dedicated to the memory of Isaac O'Brien was unveiled on behalf of the YMCA by Albert O'Brien. Mr. Rowe Harding, chairman of the West Wales AAA, said in his address, 'not only to perpetuate the memory of the name of Ike O'Brien, but also to perpetuate the great virtues of his character.'

The following week, track and field training resumed on Tuesday and Thursday at the Talbot Athletic Ground by kind permission of Aberavon RFC.

THIS MEMORIAL
IS HUNG HERE AS
A TRIBUTE TO
Isaac O'Brien
Port Talbot Y.M.C.A. Harriers
1923 _____ 1945
Who died February 11th, 1945.

He was a really great-hearted Athlete, famous in International Athletics, who brought fame to himself and great credit to his club, town and country.

His record here is some evidence of his prowess.

1st Welsh Marathon Championship, 1937-38-39.
1st West Wales Marathon Championship, 1936-37-38-39.
6th British Marathon Championship, 1936.
4th Scottish Marathon Championship, 1938.
1st Guardian Cup Race, 1925-26-27-28-29-30.

Welsh "Noteworthy Performance" 50 Miles Run
   (Llangadock—Carmarthen—Kidwelly—Swansea), 1937
   6 hours 20 minutes.

Cardiff—Swansea Run, 1938. 7 hours 40 mins.

Member of British Y.M.C.A. Athletic Team
   International Y.M.C.A. Championships, 1930, at Copenhagen.

Member of British Workers' Athletic Team
   International Workers' Olympiad, 1932, at Vienna.

" Know ye not that they which run in a race, though all run,
   only one man gains the prize? So run that ye may win "
                                                   —1st Cor. ix 24 (Weymouth)

At the Grovesend sports held in mid-June, there were some fine performances from West Wales athletes. However, there were no winners from PTYM on this occasion – you can't win them all!

On July 12th, to celebrate the upcoming Silver Anniversary of PTYMCA Harriers in October, a large crowd at the Talbot Athletic witnessed some thrilling racing and field events. The senior section had not fully recovered its membership after the war, so it was left to the juniors to uphold the honour of the club. Val Antolin won the boys 100yards, and Roy Bish won the youths 100 (10.1) and the 220 (23.7). In the open events, there were wins for D. O'Sullivan 220 (23.6), R. T. Howells 440 (54.7), Alfor Davies high jump 5 feet ½ inch and the PTYM relay team.

The following week Ken Jones (100yds) and Val Antolin (75yds Hurdles) represented Glamorgan Schools in the Inter-County Champs.

The YMCA Championships were held at Abertridwr on Saturday 27th, July. Unfortunately, there were very few senior members there and it was left to the juniors to secure a very creditable second place.

West Wales achieved a comfortable victory on August 12th at the Talbot Athletic against strong opposition from Monmouthshire and East Glamorgan. Praise was heaped on the organisers PTYM when, 'everything went without a hitch and the YMCA Harriers once again enhanced their reputation of being masters in the art of sports organization.' PTYM winners for West Wales were Len 'The fastest white man in Britain' Madden (100yds 9.9), V. Morgan (pole vault 11feet), D. W. Samuels (220 23.2), Alvo Daniels (junior long jump 19feet 8inches) and K. Jones (junior javelin 138feet 3inches).

There were some good results for PTYM athletes at the Welsh AAA Championships held in Clydach on 17th August. Fred Needs won the javelin with a throw of 123 feet 6½inches (37.66m). Roy Williams won the 440 and also the 880 in a new record time of 2minutes 6.2 seconds. Cyril Evans (pole vault) and E. M. Jenkins (shot & discus) also won their events.

1947

In February, 1947, AEW was again elected vice-president of the Welsh AAA. At this time, he was also secretary of the West Wales AAA, qualified timekeeper and field judge and a field events coach.

In early May, 1947, the club resumed training for the coming season at the Talbot Athletic ground with a good mix of young talent and older experienced athletes. Emphasis was placed on the pole vault where Cyril Evans, Welsh champion and record holder, along with AEW, would provide expert coaching (Evans' best vault of 11feet 6inches came at the White City against top class opposition). Interested parties were advised to contact secretary Mr. F. C. Payne.

The Mumbles 5-mile road race took place on 24th May, 1947. John Nash was 2nd in 25-54 and Albert O'Brien was 3rd (26-31) behind winner W. L. Raddon of Hendy in 25-45.

The Youth Club Championships took place on 12th July at the Talbot Athletic despite heavy rain setting in later in the meeting. PTYM winners were – C. Gilbertson high jump and javelin; H. Lodwig shot; A. Murray 880; J. Evans 100 and 220. PT also won the relay.

In a busy July, PTYM regained the YMCA Championship at Abertridwr and the Hendy cup at Clydach. Selection for West Wales was based on the Clydach match. PTYM athletes selected were – Len Madden 100, D. W. Samuel 220, Roy Williams and V. Snook 440, Roy Williams 880, T. Mainwaring long jump, J. F. James and T. Mainwaring hop step&jump, John Nash and D. Rees 3-miles. Amongst the juniors selected were Roy Bish, Val Antolin and Albert O'Brien.

Despite a bus strike and bad weather there was a good attendance at the Byass Works sports. The Glamorgan County 100 yards Championship was held at this meeting and it resulted in a fine race won by D. W. Samuel by only a very small margin from Roy Bish. In the open 100, T. Mainwaring showed a clean pair of heels to Samuel who could only manage 2nd place. There were good performances from B. Phillips, D. Amphlett and V. Snook in the junior section. In the girl's events, the outstanding athletes were J. Lodwig and Victrix Ludorum, Connie Pascoe of Cwmafan.

In August, 1947, Roy Williams and Val Antolin helped Glamorgan to a great win over Monmouthshire. The Welsh Marathon Championships were held at Margam with John Nash full of confidence on the start line. Unfortunately, after twenty miles of this arduous course, he was forced to retire with stomach cramps. Six runners entered, but only two finished. Martin Richards of Highgate was the winner in 3hours 28minutes.

Fielding a number of youngsters, PTYM travelled to St. Athan for a mid-week match against the RAF. The battle was bravely contested and PT went down to only a narrow defeat.

In a match at Pontardawe, young sprinter, J. Evans won both the 100 and 220. John Nash easily won the mile in 4-40.

The Youths Challenge Shield was comfortably won by PT with great efforts from J. Evans (1st 100), C. Gilbertson (2nd 220), V. Antolin (3rd 440) and D. M. Thomas was an unexpected winner of the 2-mile walk.

The club was not well represented at the West Wales Championships where Addenbrook of Swansea took Roy Williams' 440 record. Not to be outdone, Williams thundered around the track to beat his own West Wales record in the 880.

Jim Davies was selected for the Welsh cross-country team which travelled to Europe for the Tour de Spa. Wales were not humbled in a very strong international field, finishing a creditable 4th and ahead of England and Scotland.

To sum up the year of 1947, 'Spikes II' wrote this review in the Guardian: -
The athletic season just concluded must be one of the most successful in the history of the YMCA Harriers. The club, without a doubt, can claim to be ranked as the best in West Wales. Turning attention further afield, it can be safely claimed that the club ranks as one of the top three clubs in Wales. I would like to see an inter-club match next year between Newport, Roath and PTYM to settle any doubt regarding which of these three great clubs are really Wales' best all-round athletic clubs. It is most certain that the local club would be well to the fore and capable of putting up a good fight. The strength of the club is in the all-round ability of its athletes on track and in the field events.

1948

The year began with another article by Spikes II stating that this was a championship year for PTYM full of great expectations. He went on to list the fixtures the club would be hosting – Junior Cross-Country Championship, Welsh AAA Track&Field Championships, Hendy Shield and YMCA Championship. Undoubtedly an indication of the high regard of the organizational prowess of PTYM Harriers.

The Welsh Junior Cross-Country Championship held at Stormy Down on 24th January, 1948 was a triumph for PTYM. Not only was it superbly organized, but there were also splendid performances from the PT runners. In 1st place was Jim Davies, 2nd John Nash and 4th (again!) was Albert O'Brien.

An inter-club cross-country match against the Mond and Trinity College in early March at Clydach saw PT run out comfortable winners. Despite O'Brien's unavailability, the first three places were filled by Jim Davies, John Nash and D. Rees.

Sickness and work commitments meant that only six runners turned out for the Welsh Senior XC Championships at Caerleon in March, 1948. The exceptionally strong field contained a large number of exiles from top clubs, which was an extra burden for the weakened PT team. Added to that was the fact that the rules stated a team had to consist of six finishers. Less than that number and the team would not count. This meant that all the PT team had to finish the race. Jim Davies was well to the fore again placing 5th, Nash 15th and Rees 20th, On the fourth of five laps, Albert O'Brien had trouble with his spikes which he discarded, running the last lap bare-footed to finish a brave 35th. D. Nunn was 43rd and C. Wright 44th to give PTYM 4th team overall.

CLUB WITH A WEALTH OF TALENT

THE Y.M.C.A. HARRIERS

The Port Talbot Y.M.C.A. Harriers are to-day making a name for themselves in the world of athletics, and are looking forward to an even brighter and more successful future. The club, one of the finest in the Principality, has a wealth of talent at its disposal, including champions in various athletic events. Its members are now busy organising the annual Welsh A.A.A. Championships to be held in Port Talbot in June. Above is a section of the club—the cross-country team which took part in the recent Welsh Senior Cross-Country Championships. Back row (left to right): F. C. Payne, hon. secretary; D. Nunn, J. Nash, I. Hopkins, team manager; C. T. Evans, Welsh pole vault record holder, and Jim Davies, Welsh cross-country international, the club's newest and probably most talented acquisition in years. Front row (left to right): C. Wright, A. O'Brien (son of the famous late Isaac O'Brien, who is following in his father's foootsteps), A. E. Williams, secretary of West Wales Executive of the A.A.A., and D. Rees. These are some of the athletes and organisers who will be asking for your support for the Welsh Championships in June.

The Mumbles road race was an eagerly awaited event in March, 1948. Club secretary, Fred Payne, had high hopes of bettering the previous year's success of Nash 2nd and O'Brien 3rd. In splendid form, Jim Davies led from the gun and was 250 yards ahead of 2nd placed Nash when he crossed the finish line inside St. Helen's Stadium in a course record of 23 minutes 39 1/2 seconds. Nash was roundly applauded by the huge crowd for his sportsmanship when he ran straight to Davies to congratulate him. The large contingent of Aberavon supporters were delighted at this double victory after they had just seen their club beat Swansea RFC. O'Brien was 4th (again!) and Rees 5th which gave PTYM the team trophy by a huge margin.

For the first time ever the Welsh AAA Track&Field Championships were held at the Talbot Athletic Ground on June 16th, 1948. Heavy early morning rain made for soggy conditions. However, the sun soon had his hat on and the day's programme went without a hitch. A strong wind blew the hurdles over, but assisted the sprinters. 'Taken all-in-all, the meeting was a success and a happy one for all concerned, the spectators particularly enjoying a wonderful afternoon's sport in splendid surroundings, thanks to the generosity of the Aberavon RFC who placed their Athletic Ground at the disposal of the local YMCA Harriers.' The shock of the day was the defeat of veteran D. J. P. 'Dai' Richards who was overtaken in the finishing straight of the 2-mile walk by T. L. Owens (Manchester). As expected, Welsh wing-threequarter, Ken Jones of Newport retained his 100 (9.9) and 220 (23.1) titles beating Len Madden and K. Maddocks of PTYM in the shorter race. Other PT athletes competing were Cyril Evans (pole vault 1st, 10 feet 6inches), A. Davies (2nd, long jump), John Nash (3rd, 3-miles). There were also some promising performances from the younger members – V. Morgan (1st Boy's 100 10.1), C. Gilbertson (1st Youth's 100 10.2), Roy Bish (1st Junior 100 10.9) and G. Venables (1st 880 2mins 12.4 secs).

July, 1948 was another busy month for PTYM. The Hendy Shield match took place on the 8th at the Talbot Athletic, where PT were convincing winners yet again. Unfortunately, K. Madocks was injured in the 100 and only just managed to limp across the line. This injury also caused him to lose his Welsh vest at Abertillery the following Saturday.

A week later, there were some fine athletic performances at the Steel Company of Wales Gala Day. Surprise of the day was Cyril Evans' defeat in the pole vault by Aircraftsman Akonen of Poland who was based at RAF St. Athan. Both athletes cleared 10feet 5inches, but Akonen had one less failure than Evans. Junior athlete, Clive Gilbertson also claimed a major scalp when he beat Len Madden in the open handicap 100. His start of eight yards was just a little too much for Madden to overtake. Madden went on to win the open 100 comfortably.

The YMCA Championships were hosted by PT on 24th July, but this time at the Cwmafan Welfare Ground. 'Abertridwr put up a strong challenge, but the Harriers met and stifled every opposition successfully', to win the John Llewellyn Cup for the tenth time. There were significant performances from junior Clive Gilbertson 1st 100, 220 and long jump and the experienced Cyril Evans 1st pole vault, high jump, hop step and jump.

A fine display of athletics was provided for local enthusiasts at the Talbot Athletic when West Wales met a talented London United Hospitals team on 7th August, 1948. As was expected, the meeting attained a high standard pf prowess and several Welsh all-comers records were broken. It was not surprising therefore, that the Hospitals team ran out easy winners. After the match, the visitors were the guests of honour at a dinner in the Walnut Tree Hotel. Later, they all attended the usual weekly dance at the YMCA.

The summer season of 1948 was a somewhat disappointing one. PTYM had to field weakened teams on several occasions due to illness and work commitments. Despite this, the Hendy Shield and the Llewellyn Cup were both retained.

At the AGM, AEW remarked that 'The period of difficult organization after the war had now passed and the club in 1947/48 had enjoyed a very full and successful season, proving that this club was a force to be reckoned with in the Welsh athletic world. The objective should now be to build up in numbers and standard, and he felt that, in spite of the past good record it had to its credit, the best was yet to come.' The following officials were elected – G. M. Hapgood, chairman; AEW, vice-chairman; F. C. Payne, secretary; C. T. Evans, captain; J. Nash, vice-captain; G. T. Overton, L. Aitken, K. Davidson, W. Owen and A. Murray, committee.

In March, 1949 the British YMCA XC International in Glasgow was of special interest to local sportsmen because the Welsh team was composed entirely of PTYM Harriers. John Nash and Albert O'Brien finished 7th and 8th and the Welsh team was 3rd. After the race the athletes were taken on a trip to Loch Lomond.

The popular Mumbles road race was once again held in April 1949. Although fielding a weakened team, PTYM again provided the winner. John Nash delighted the hundreds of Aberavon RFC supporters at St. Helen's when he entered the stadium just after Aberavon had defeated Swansea.

In May 1949, Spikes commented that 'athletes for the 1949 track season are now getting off the mark'. He went on to list a number of the season's events which included the Hendy Shield and the YMCA Championships. PTYM also had the honour of hosting the Welsh AAA Junior Championships. Spikes added that PTYM had developed into one of the main centres of athletics in Wales and had done a tremendous amount to develop athletics in the Principality.

There was a surprising defeat for Len Madden in the 100 at the Glamorgan Championships on the 4th of June. He was beaten by the unknown Cardiff sprinter, R. Parry who won in the modest time of 10.5. Port Talbot's R. E. Thomas made up for this disappointment by winning the 220. This report concluded by saying that surely the Port Talbot Municipal Council could give some hope to its athletes that a sorely needed track would be built in the near future.

John Nash, in training for the Welsh marathon, did well to finish 3rd in the Welsh 3-mile Championship at Abertillery in late June.

It was also noted in a report of 1st of July that D. J. P. 'Dai' Richards had definitely retired after twenty-seven continuous years of competition and winning dozens of Welsh championships and records. Truly a remarkable athlete.

There were many sterling performances at the Junior Welsh AAA Championships at the Talbot Athletic Ground on July 2nd. The athletics was superb, but Spikes had this to say about the lack of supporters, 'I don't feel very proud of my fellow townsmen, who, with very few exceptions, failed to support one of the most important meetings in Wales. It is not a good excuse that the weather was so good, that the beach was more tempting. One individual who prides himself on his knowledge of athletics had the presumption to tell me – 'only a kid's sports'. Kid's sports, forsooth! These 18 and 19-year-olds need all the encouragement they can get if they are to develop into potential Olympic athletes'. A look at the results of this meeting show that there were sixteen records broken.

A 3-club match planned for Tuesday 12th July at the Talbot Athletic was marred by the non-appearance of the Mond team. There was still a keen competition between PTYM and RAF St. Athan in which a weakened home team finished a close second. There were wins for W. H. Parton in the senior 100 and 220, Ray Jones in the junior javelin and W. Kelly in the long jump.

The major event of the SCoW sports on 9th July was the Welsh Marathon Championships. The race had only nine entrants, started and finished at the Margam fields and followed a route through Port Talbot, Briton Ferry, Skewen, Llansamlet and back. A new feature of this race was the introduction of radio communication on its progress. Spectators on the field were kept informed by wireless from an armoured car of the 282 Field Squadron Royal Engineers Territorial Army which followed the race. Ken Thomas of Newport won in 2-54 while John Nash and Albert O'Brien failed to finish.

South Wales avenged the previous year's heavy defeat by London Hospitals by gaining a narrow, but well-deserved victory on 16th July at the Talbot Athletic. Highlight of the afternoon was the performance of Ray Jones, junior javelin champion. Jones rose to the occasion with a mighty throw of 172feet 1inch (52.46m). The mayor of Port Talbot, Alderman D. H. Davies JP, thanked the officials and organizers of PTYM and hoped that this meeting would be the forerunner of many more in the future.

In August, 1949, there were several successes for PTYM athletes in the West Wales Championships at St. Helen's John Nash dictated the pace of the 3-mile race and won in a new record time of 15-47.2. Ken Patten won the youths 100 in 10.9. D. W. Kelly won the hop step and jump with a leap of 41feet 11½inches (12.80m). PTYM also won the 4x110 relay race by inches from Swansea Vale.

For some unknown reason, there was a lack of information available for the remainder of 1949, so there ends the account of the 1940s.

1950s

John Nash scored a magnificent victory in the Welsh Novice XC Championships at Llantarnam on 21st January, 1950. This was a step up from the previous year when he finished second behind clubmate Jim Davies. Albert O'Brien was 6th, W. Burns 17th, G. R. Evans 67th and W. Charles 70th giving PTYM 5th place in the team event.

Three nominations were received for the office of president of the Welsh AAA in February, 1950. One of those was AEW. The citation stated, 'Mr. Williams has had much to do with the modern development of athletics in Wales – coaching and lecturing on athletics – and he has contributed much to the press and national magazines for years. He is kept busy during the year as an official at athletic meetings throughout Wales and has been judge or timekeeper in London and other English centres. A foundation member of his club when it was formed in 1921, he has seen many of his fellow members achieve many distinctions in team competitions. He is proud of the fact that the name and reputation of Port Talbot YMCA Harriers is well-known as much in England as in Wales.'

It was not to be for AEW this time. When the ballot papers were counted, Cyril Howell, the serving secretary of the WAAA topped the poll.

There was consolation for AEW in May, however. He was elected a life vice-president of WAAA, 'For long and valued service to amateur athletics in West Wales. He initiated the movement in 1932 which led to the complete reorganization of athletics in Wales, culminating in 1948 in Wales becoming a separate entity in British Athletics.' Expressing his gratitude at this honour, AEW also said that Port Talbot deserved to have a sports stadium of its own, where athletes could train, coaches could impart technique and competition could be properly presented to the public.

Despite steady and depressing rain from the middle of the afternoon, the Glamorgan County Championships held at the Talbot Athletic on 27th June were deemed a complete success. There were wins in the junior events for J. C. Phillips (high jump) and E. Morgan in the hop, step and jump. John Nash won the senior 3-miles and Albert O'Brien was 3rd.

The first annual sports of RTB held at the Talbot Athletic on 1st July were blessed with ideal conditions. The winner of the junior 880 yards by a large margin was a youngster named Jim O'Brien – following in the footsteps of his famous father, Isaac.

There were three Welsh Championship events included in the Steel Company of Wales sports on the 8th of July. The highlight of these was the marathon where Tom Richards, runner-up in the Olympics, was due to run. True to form, Richards won in 2hours 42 mins 53secs, but didn't have an easy ride. There was stern competition from John Nash who ran bravely for second place in 2-44.23. Both men were inside Ike O'Brien's pre-war record of 2-45.00. Derek Cole, the army champion born in Taibach, broke Cyril Evans' Welsh pole vault record with a height of 11feet 31/4 inches (3.44m).

There were no PTYM athletes in the South Wales team to face the London United Hospitals at the Talbot Athletic Ground on 22nd July, 1950. It was notable, however, for the appearance of Arthur Wint, the 440 Olympic champion. His attempt at a Welsh all-comers record of 49.8 was spoiled by steady rain all afternoon and he could only manage 50.4. The South Wales team won the match which was ample compensation for the sodden crowd.

A three-cornered match between PTYM, Bridgend Grammar School Old Boys and Neath Harriers took place at the Talbot Athletic on 25th July. John Nash easily won the 3-miles by a lap and a half and PTYM were comfortable winners of the team event.

The following article was published by AEW on 11th August – 'Over a long period of years Port Talbot has been gradually developing its athletics to the present day, when it is now one of the chief, if not the premier centre in Wales. This has been helped tremendously by the Aberavon Rugby Club, which has always been ready to place its facilities at the convenience of PTYM. Among local athletes who have taken the name of Port Talbot into the wider field of athletics are D. J. P. Richards, Cyril Evans, Will Owen, Isaac O'Brien, Roy Williams, Len Madden and John Nash who are first class performers. I am sure that we are proud of their prowess and hope that among the youth of Port Talbot there are those who will continue to achieve fame, which we hope to share in.'

On October 11th, 1950, Port Talbot Ex-Service-Men's Club held the inaugural Ike O'Brien Memorial Race from their HQ in Cwmafan Road. There were only seven entrants which included John Nash and Albert O'Brien who took an early lead. Nash took over the lead in Pantdu and was a comfortable winner in 39-02, with O'Brien finishing 4th. After the race the runners and officials were entertained to tea, and trophies were presented by the mayor Alderman T. I. Rees JP.

The 29th AGM of PTYM took place in October, 1950. Kenneth Davison, team manager, stated that the club had achieved considerable success, pointing out that club captain, John Nash, had been in outstanding form. Women's athletics was discussed and it was decided to form a Women's Section. The following officers were elected: – Chairman - AEW; Vice-chair - George Hapgood; Secretary and Treasurer - W. K. A. Lang; Team Manager - Kenneth Davison; Coach – Aubrey Hibbs; Captain – John Nash; Vice-captain – Cyril Evans; Committee – W. Owen, Leslie Aitken, J. T. Fisher, G. Overton and Emrys James.

The Welsh Novices XC Championships were held at SCoW fields on 9th December, 1950. D. J. P. Richards junior made a brave attempt to emulate his famous father in winning this race, but had to be content with 3rd place. It was a disappointing day for PTYM who couldn't raise a team. The Welsh XC Association praised PTYM for the organization and facilities at the venue.

1951

In March, 1951, John Nash was unlucky to just miss out on a place in the Welsh XC team. He finished in 11th place at the Senior Championships and only the first 10 were selected. Nash put aside his disappointment to help PT win the Welsh YMCA XC Championships the following week in Rhoose. He was the individual winner on the 7½-mile course in 42-35. Albert O'Brien was 3rd, W. J. Thomas 6th and these three were selected for the Welsh YMCA team against England, Ireland and Scotland.

On 2nd June, PT members stepped up to the mark at the West Wales Championships in Clydach. There were wins for John Collins (440yds), Eiran Morgan (hop, step & jump), W. J. Thomas (880) and John Nash (3 miles). All were selected for Swansea and District in a match against Cardiff & District and Newport & District.

Also, in June, 1951, it was interesting to note that, following the lead of PTYM, a Welsh Women's AAA was formed.

The district match with Cardiff and Newport took place on 16th June. The PT athletes did themselves credit against strong opposition. John Collins ran superbly to win the 440 in 53.0, beating Welsh champion Gwyn Murphy.

AEW reported that there were several important meetings to be staged in Port Talbot over the summer season. He added that, 'If ever there was a need in Port Talbot for a first-class athletic stadium it is now, as athletes have developed considerably, and our athletes train and compete under conditions which do not help them to produce their best. So, roll on the day when we can put athletics over in its right setting!'

The annual SCoW sports took place on 7th July, 1951 at Margam playing fields. This meeting was a little special because D. J. P. Richards junior took part. He was 2nd in the 1-mile and won the 880-yds. In the senior races, John Collins, noted for his prowess as a 440 man, won the 880 in the astonishing time of 1-53.9! The main event again was the Welsh Marathon Championship. The winner was Horace Oliver (Reading) in a new Welsh record of 2hrs 42.0mins. John Nash battled bravely for 2nd place for the second year running.

The YMCA T&F Championships were held at the Talbot Athletic on 21st July. PTYM (who lost out to Carmarthen in 1950) were at full strength and easily won the competition. For the first time ever, PT fielded a women's team who did rather well. Rhona Heekman won the 100 yds in 13.1 with Rita Evans second. The tables were turned in the 220 when Rita Evans won in 26.4. John Nash was beaten by a whisker on the line in the mile, but comfortably won the 3-miles in 15-35.4.

John (also known as Jack) Nash featured in an article published on 17th August, 1951. His teammates had noticed that he seemed to suffer cramp after 20 miles or more of running. They decided something was wrong and sent him to an osteopath in Penarth. It seems his hip was out of joint which had caused the displacement of three vertebrae, making his right leg one incher shorter than his left. The problem was rectified and it was hoped Nash would soon return to full fitness.

Although at times the rain teamed down, the match between South Wales and London United Hospitals was completed without a hitch. A thrilling sprint saw John Collins get the verdict against English champion O. Williams in the 440, both being given 53.0. An innovation was introduced at this meeting. A PT Youth Clubs v PT Grammar Schools match which, it was hoped, would encourage the youth of the district to take up athletics. John Nash was still recovering from his treatment, but was determined to complete his planned 33-mile run from Cardiff to Newport, carrying letters from the mayor of Cardiff to the mayor of PT. In his support party was timekeeper Alf Yeomans and brothers Albert, Jim and John O'Brien. There was great interest shown in this cavalcade along the way. One witty cyclist shouted, 'Why don't you buy a bike!' Shortly after, Nash passed the same cyclist repairing a puncture and found the breath to retort, 'Why don't you buy a pair of daps!' After 3hrs 56mins, he arrived at the Talbot ground to tumultuous applause and was presented with a Festival of Britain medal to mark his achievement. Incidentally, S. Wales beat the Hospital comfortably by 68 pts – 28 pts.

One of the most thrilling finishes to a race ever seen in Port Talbot came in the second Ike O'Brien Memorial Race on 17th November. Ten runners started, John Nash and John Edwards (Carmarthen) setting a swift pace to Pontrhydyfen and returning along to Ynysygwas where they were caught by Albert O'Brien and Tom Woods (Newport). There was nothing separating these four runners as they came in sight of the finish. Nash made a desperate dash for the line and was just ahead of O'Brien, Woods and Edwards with only a few feet between the four.

1952

PTYM was honoured to host the Welsh AAA AGM at the YMCA on 26th January, 1952. It was reported that there were 103 affiliated clubs and a full programme of events had been prepared for Welsh athletics.

A new innovation was trialled by PTYM members in February, 1952. The Americans had been using weight training for some years to improve their all-round fitness with good results. The emphasis was on training, not weight lifting – exercising with weights.

Several PT athletes competed with distinction in the Hoover sports in May. John Nash comfortably won the 3-mile in 15-50.7. John Collins won both his heat in 53.8 and the final of the 440 in 51.9 against strong opposition. The junior team won the 4x110 relay in 46.9.

The Coop Society held its sports at the Talbot Athletic on 21st June. The main feature was a 5-mile race starting at Victoria Gardens, Neath and finishing at the Talbot ground. Favourite for the race was John Nash who, unfortunately, had a bad day at the office. He could only manage 5th place and collapsed, exhausted over the finish line. There was some good running from the PT athletes including a win for D. Gilbertson in the junior 100yds. The West Wales Women's 100yds Championship was held at this meeting and was won by Rita Evans with B. Partleton 2nd.

Brilliant running by Welshman, Tom Richards (S. London Harriers) was the highlight of the SCoW sports on 12th July. He galloped home in the marathon in a new Welsh record of 2hrs 30mins 40secs. Ever the proverbial bridesmaid, John Nash finished 2nd for the third year in a row, but was ecstatic to record a new personal best of 2hrs 35mins 43secs. D. Gilbertson won the junior 100 and Rita Evans was second in the women's 220yds. The excitement continued for the spectators with many close finishes on track and field. In moments of relaxation the fair and refreshment tents did a good trade.

There were more records set up at the Inter-Counties Youth Championships at the Talbot Athletic than have ever been seen in Port Talbot before, for, as this was the first event of its kind, every performance was a record! Some of the local winners were Glen Landeg - hop,step&jump (39ft 1/2inch) and javelin (158ft 3inch); Carwen Edwards – girls long jump (14ft 8inch).

The Hendy Shield match took place on 2nd August. A below par PT team could only finish 2nd behind an improving Neath club. Winners for PTYM were K. Thomas Junior 100 (10.6); John Collins senior 440 (56.4); C. K. Fletcher pole vault (10ft 0ins); P. Stevens high jump (5ft 3ins). The PTYM juniors won the relay again.

At the Welsh T&F Championships in Maindy Stadium, John Collins brought home the 440yds gold medal (51.7) and PT exile Dyfrig Rees (Coventry Godiva), ran superbly to win both the 2M steeplechase (11-21.1) and the 3-mile (15-18.2).

John Collins, Welsh 440 yards Champion (51.7), 1952

Bryn Thomas, in his 'Sporting Chatter' noted that Val Antolin was commencing his teacher training at Loughborough College. Antolin had trials for both Welsh soccer and rugby teams. He chose soccer and was capped against Ireland. He was also Welsh Secondary Schools

hurdles and javelin champion.

The third running of the Ike Memorial race took place on 29th November, 1952. The organisers included a team prize which attracted a field of 14 runners. A 50-mph gale lashed the runners with rain and sleet as they set off up Cwmafan Road to Pontrhydydfen. Norman

Wilson (RAF St. Athan) led from the start and couldn't be overhauled. John Nash was 4th; Albert O'Brien 11th and the RAF won the team trophy.

1953

Very little information can be found about 1953. John Nash continued to plug away. He picked up bronze medals for 3rd place in both the Welsh Marathon (2-50.30) and the Welsh 3-mile (15-42.9). W. E. Manning also picked up 2 bronze Welsh Championship medals in the 110yd hurdles and 440yd hurdles.

1954

The Welsh YMCA XC championships were held at Rhoose on 13th February, 1954. The first six home would be chosen for the Welsh team and a further three would be added at the selector's discretion. John Nash had a comfortable lead when he saw a junior runner collapse. He had no hesitation in picking up the youngster and carrying him to the changing rooms. Nash resumed the race and finished 10th. To the selector's credit Nash was still named in the Welsh YMCA team.

In June, 1954, John Collins commented about the lack of athletic facilities in Port Talbot. The Aberavon wing and PTYM quarter miler said there was a working arrangement between the Harriers and Aberavon RFC, but the ground was not ideal and was not always available for the athletes.

The weather was so bad on the 17th July that all the T&F events at the SCoW sports were cancelled. The only event which took place was the Welsh Marathon. Dyfrig Rees, a native of Cwmafan, but a member of Coventry Godiva and John Nash led the field for 18 miles. Nash then had trouble with his shoes and discarded them. He didn't give up though. He ran the rest of the race bare-footed. Rees won in 2-23.02 and Nash was second (for the 4th time!) in 2-45.58.

In October 1954, AEW stressed the importance of coaching for athletes. He gave dates for a course for coaches to be given by Empire Games champion Jim Alford at Neath Grammar School.

In January 1955, AEW was again nominated for president of WAAA. At this time, he had been secretary of the West Wales AAA for 22 years, but didn't win the election.

A common theme seemed to be surfacing amongst the sportsmen of Port Talbot. Bryn Thomas commented on the fact that the town council had spent enormous sums developing the beach, but there was still a lack of adequate sporting facilities in the town.

In March, John Nash led the YMCA XC championships until he mistimed a ditch and fell waste deep into muddy water. After first aid treatment he finished the race well down the field. He was again selected with the honour of captaining the Welsh YMCA team.

Superbly organized by Gerald Lane, the Port Talbot Schools Sports were held at the Talbot Athletic in June. The borough engineer, Gordon Griffiths was in attendance and remarked that the provision of playing fields had not been over-looked.

The Welsh Championships took place at Maindy Stadium in July. John Collins was 2nd in the 440yds (52.3) and John Nash 3rd (for a change!) in the marathon (2-54.59).

In contrast to the previous year, bright sunshine and blue skies greeted the athletes and the 4000 crowd at the SCoW games. There were two events for ladies included for the first time, for which there were no PT entrants. John Collins won the Works 220 yds and was 2nd in the open 440. D. B. Thomas won the open 100yds and a wonderful time was had by all!

The popular London United Hospitals paid their sixth visit to the Talbot Athletic on 23rd July. This time the winning team would be presented with the 'Chidzoy Trophy' kindly donated by Major Wally Chidzoy. Two Welsh all-comers records were set during the afternoon. G. Howell (Hospitals) won the 7-mile walk in 54mins 10.3 secs and K. Huckle won the 2-mile run in 9-24.2. John Collins was an easy winner of the 440. There were several junior and lady's events, the highlight of which was the win by P. Doyle of Glanafan Grammar School in the women's 100yds. During a break in the athletics a physical culture display was given by 63-year-old Mr. Percy Hunt. The Chidzoy Trophy was awarded to S. Wales who won the match by 64pts to 50.

There were some promising youngsters coming through during the summer season. Byron Thomas won the Youth Clubs Championship 100 in 10.0 and Keith Davitte won the Welsh Junior 120yds hurdles Championship in 16.4.

At the 34th AGM of the club in November, 1955, it was decided to make a special effort to revive the cross-country team which had suffered a severe blow when John Nash, the section's mainstay, had emigrated to New Zealand.

John Nash, 4-times runner-up Welsh Marathon Champs, 1950-52, 1954

1956

There was very little athletics information available in 1956. In April Alderman Llewellyn Heycock organized a rugby match between Welsh Academicals and London United Hospitals at the Talbot Athletic ground. The aim was to raise money for the 1958 Empire Games in Cardiff.

The ninth SCoW games took place on a wet and windy July day. For PTYM, Keith Davitte won the 120yds hurdles in 16.5 and John Collins was 3rd in the 220. There was one race for ladies won by C. M. Davies (Newport). No PT ladies took part.

There were just two high spots in 1956. Keith Davitte's second consecutive win in the Welsh Junior 120yds hurdles Championship and PTYM won the Welsh XC Championship.

1957

The AGM was held in March 1957. AEW was elected chairman and E. R. Patten secretary. Committee: - W. R. Johnson, G. M. Hapgood, C. T. Evans, L. Aitken, K. Davison, J. T. Fisher, A. A. Hussell and G. Lewis.

In April the club started twice a week weight training in preparation for the coming T&F season.

The Glamorgan County Championships were held at Maindy Stadium in May, 1957. George Hapwood won the high jump. In the junior events, Joyce Wheeler won the high jump, Wendy Watson the long jump and Denzil Ryan the boy's long jump. Pat Doyle was 2nd in the 100 and long jump.

Only two athletes turned up for pre-season training. By the end of June that had soared to more than 40. At the Welsh Championships, PT had the distinction of winning the Women's 4x110yds relay. The team was – Pat Doyle, Adrienne Jones, Joan Lewis and Keitha Williams.

The SCoW sports had become an important, high-class event over the years. In July, 1957 it incorporated the Welsh Junior Championships and a Welsh AAA versus AAA match. The AAA completely overwhelmed the Welsh team and the only local representative, Keith Davitte, was unable to compete.

The Hendy Shield match took place in July resulting in a comfortable win for PTYM. John Collins was the star performer, winning both the 440yds and 880. He also anchored the winning men's relay team. There were sprint races for ladies in which PTYM won the 4x110yds relay.

AEW had the honour of being selected as a field judge for an international match between GB and France in August 1957. In the same month Roy Bish and Ray Jones qualified as coaches after attending a course at Loughborough College.

PTYM held their annual dinner and dance in October during which the German Burgomasters group was introduced to the members. In his speech Dr. Dambacher spoke of the future unity of mankind which he hoped sport would promote. The highlight of the evening was the presentation of the Hendy Cup accepted on behalf of the club by John Collins.

In a two-club XC event at Gnoll Park on 16th November, Neath retained their unbeaten record. For PT, W. J. Thomas was 2nd, Jim O'Brien 4th and Albert O'Brien 7th.

The good news from abroad was that John Nash had established himself as a popular and successful 'veteran' in his new home of Wellington, New Zealand.

PTYM were the organisers of the Welsh Novice XC Championships at SCoW, Margam on 7th December. Winner of the race was W. Hotchkiss of Cardiff University. Sadly, there were no PT runners in the top twenty. On the brighter side, Miss Ann Mogford was elected to the executive committee of the Welsh Women's AAA.

1958

Early in 1958 the Welsh AAA held a course for coaches at Glanafan Grammar School. Also, in January, Charles Wright, secretary of PT and West Glam AAA was awarded a Meritorious Plaque of Honour for services to Welsh Athletics.

Four PT officials were invited to take part in the Empire Games in Cardiff later in the year. AEW was joined by Charles Wright, George Hapgood and J. Fisher. The club's capabilities were obviously highly regarded by the Games committee.

The Welsh YMCA XC Championships were held at Rhoose in March, 1958. Another O'Brien, Aneurin, ran superbly for 2nd place in the junior race. In the senior race, big brother

Jim finished 7th and was selected for the Welsh YM team. At the British YM Championships in Manchester the following month Jim placed 7th and helped Wales to win the team title.

Atrocious weather was blamed for the poor performances in the Glamorgan County Championships at the Talbot Athletic on 10th May, 1958. Jim O'Brien was 2nd in the 3-miles; D. A. Morgan 2nd in the discus and PTYM were 3rd in the women's 4x110yds relay. Joyce Wheeler set a new championship record in the high jump.

On July 18th, a team of Harriers carried the Queen's message enclosed in a silver baton as part of a relay team before the start of the Empire Games in Cardiff. Carriers of the baton were – Jim and Aneurin O'Brien, John Collins, Geraint Morgan, Alan Tanner, Glyn Williams, Elwyn Morgan, Moelwyn Jones, Derek Jones and Ieuan Prosser.

Geraint Morgan remembers that the team were offered positions as field stewards or tickets for the whole of the games. Geraint chose the tickets and, being an amateur, had to pay for them.

Running tracks were rare in those days. Most athletic competitions took place on grass tracks traced out on rugby fields. Geraint Morgan tells of the time when he was second in an 880yards race at Bargoed RFC. It was more like a XC race with a 'stream' of water near the half way line!

The Port Talbot District Youth Sports held in June at the Talbot Athletic resulted in a win for PTYM. No individuals were named, only the clubs.

1959

AEW was elected president of the Welsh AAA for the first time at their AGM in January, 1959. He was also elected to the Empire Games Council for Wales.

The SCoW playing fields at Margam proved to be an excellent venue for the Welsh Junior XC Championships. Jim O'Brien just failed to catch winner B. Perkins (Newport) but was well pleased with 2nd place.

In a keenly contested XC match with Roath Harriers at Seven Sisters, West Glamorgan ran out winners by just 6 points. The remarkable fact about this event was that it was the first time all four O'Brien brothers had run together in a representative match. Jim won the race, Aneurin 5th, Albert 8th and John 11th. Harry O'Brien was yet to make his debut.

In the Welsh YMCA XC Championships held in Rhoose on 21st March, Jim O'Brien led all the way, but was pipped on the post by Ron Franklin of Newport. David Townsend and Aneurin O'Brien found the lack of spikes a great handicap in the Youth's race, but still managed to finish 3rd and 4th. Jim was selected for the Welsh YMCA team for the international at Kinmel Park, Rhyl. He was the first Welsh runner to finish in 6th place overall and the Welsh team was 2nd behind England.

PTYM, in something of an experiment, organized a series of road relays on 25th April, 1959. Starting and finishing in Broad Street, the runners took to the pavements of the surrounding streets in torrential rain. In the Youth's race, Clive Arnold ran a determined last leg to bring home the Dyffryn Grammar School team in 1st place. Jim O'Brien ran the fastest leg of the day to help the senior team win their section.

A most ambitious programme of events was witnessed by probably the largest crowd ever gathered in Port Talbot on 8th August 1959. A series of relays and a 10-mile walking race were included, but the marathon, on a 6-lap course around Sandfields Estate, was undoubtedly the highlight. Jim O'Brien was well in contention until at 20 miles knee trouble forced him to drop out. The race was won by Rhys Davies (Coventry Godiva) in 2-34.25.

1960s

In January, 1960, the honour of being president of the Welsh AAA was bestowed on AEW for the second year in succession.

There were high hopes that Jim O'Brien would win the Welsh YMCA XC Championships and be the first of his family to bring home the 'Isaac O'Brien Cup'. Jim took an early lead, but lost ground after a heavy fall and finished 2nd to Ron Franklyn (Newport). John O'Brien claimed 4th place, David Townsend 6th and all three were selected for the Welsh YM team.

A meeting between PTYM and Port Talbot Council in March agreed to hold the Aberavon Promenade races on 20th August. It was also decided to hold a new event - a footballer's relay race.

Readers were advised that coaching was commencing at PTYM gym. Coach, Jeffery Harris was doing an excellent job at the circuit and weight training sessions.

In April, 1960, in order to raise funds for the club, a film of the 1958 Empire Games in Cardiff was to be shown in the YM gym.

There are ups and downs in life and there is no exception in athletics. The organisers at PTYM were reluctantly forced to cancel the road relays planned for May because of insufficient entries.

Jim O'Brien was in outstanding form at the Welsh 3-miles Championship at Abertillery in July, 1960. World class athlete, John Merriman, was the winner, but Jim's gritty running earned him 2nd place.

In early August, entries were coming in steadily for the Promenade Races. The footballer's relay was proving a popular event, the first team to enter being Carleon Training College RFC. The marathon course was designed with spectators in mind. Starting on Princess Margaret Way, there was a small loop of 1 mile 385 yards followed by five 5-mile laps of Sandfields estate. A novelty event was also to be included – prizes were offered for the first three in an OAP 1-mile walking race. At this stage there was only one entrant!

Came the day and there were fourteen starters in the marathon, including Jim, Albert and John O'Brien. However, they didn't make the top three and Jim had to drop out with ligament trouble. J. R. Bratt of Tipton Harriers won. The footballer's relay was won by Newport RFC, Aberavon RFC finished 3rd. The OAP's walk did take place and was won by Councilor William Jones – 86 years old!

Jim made a swift recovery from his injury and won both the 1-mile and 2-mile Road Runners Club Championships at Mountain Ash.

It was envisaged in October, 1960 that a sports stadium at Port Talbot would cost about £25,000. The stadium would include a running track of 440yards and a cycle track around the outside of 500 yards. It would cost another £15-20,000 for a stand. AEW appealed for positive action to implement the plan.

Port Talbot Harriers and Athletic Club

All was quiet in January, 1961. Then, a bombshell burst at the PTYM AGM on Tuesday 7th February, 1961 – AEW resigned from the club! He stated as his reason, *'My resignation is a protest against the policy of the board of management of the Port Talbot YMCA which typifies an attitude of ingratitude and disloyalty to the past – and against a policy which neglects its oldest agency, the Harriers Club. Facilities have been withdrawn which the Harriers rightly feel they should be allowed in the development of their training. There have been instances when the gymnasium at the YMCA was not available to members of the Harriers because of a card party – described as a bridge convention. But for the grace of the Glamorgan Education Authority who have afforded us facilities, the club would have folded up years ago. I have fought over the years to keep this club in being and anything I have accomplished in the administration of athletics at national level I hold to the loyalty of members of the Harriers. The Harriers had been denied the gym facilities on many other occasions.'*

AEW also said it was impossible to carry on the Harriers agency in those conditions and as a result he was resigning from the Harriers agency. AEW then left the meeting and the whole committee stood down en bloc.

On Thursday 9th February, 1961, a public meeting chaired by the mayor, councilor W. E. Paisley JP, was held at the Port Talbot Municipal Buildings. After the mayor had gone into the purpose of the meeting, AEW outlined the history of athletics in Port Talbot and emphasized the fact that the Harriers were rated the 3rd best club in Wales. He hoped that the meeting would agree to set up the new club and he was prepared to start building it anew. His remarks were greeted with acclamation and the resolution was read by Geoffrey Pipes, a pupil at Glanafan Grammar School. The resolution stated – 'That this meeting approve that the Port Talbot Harriers and Athletic Club be formed to develop and encourage the youth of the Borough of Port Talbot and surrounding districts to take part in amateur athletics.' The resolution was carried unanimously. The committee was elected as follows – Chairman – Frank Pipes, Secretary – AEW, Treasurer – George Hapgood, Assistant Secretary – Val Antolin, Women's Secretary – Miss M. J. Wilson. The general committee was – Idwal Hopkin, Will Owen, C. J. Williams, Les Aitken, W. Johnson, Sam Davies, Ken Jones, V. Wehrle, Tom Lewis, Mrs Mainwaring, Miss Wilson, Miss L. Evans, Jim O'Brien and Geoffrey Pipes. The meeting also decided that the club colours would be a black vest with a 4-inch-wide red chest band and black shorts.

In effect, nothing had changed. The club had merely changed its name from Port Talbot YMCA Harriers to Port Talbot Harriers and Athletic Club.

It was straight back to business for Jim O'Brien. The Welsh XC Championships were held in Seven Sisters at the end of February. Despite losing his way twice, Jim still won the race with the greatest of ease to become Welsh 7-mile XC Champion.

In March, 1961 the club started training at Dyffryn Grammar School gym under coach Jeff Harris. Sessions for men were on Tuesday and Wednesday, while the ladies met on Friday. It was also planned to set up an Athletics Coaching Centre in Port Talbot with qualified coaches in attendance.

Bryn Thomas reported in the May edition of his column that the superb junior athlete, Andrea Magdalino, was resident in Hong Kong and still active in athletics.

Inspired by seeing Herb Elliot win the 880-yds and 1-mile at the 1958 Commonwealth Games in Cardiff, Dillwyn Robbins decided that running was the sport for him. He started training on 1st June, 1959. He was a dedicated athlete and kept meticulous records of all his training runs and races. Dil, as he was affectionately known, later joined PTH, but was determined not to run a race until he was satisfied that he was fit enough to perform well. That day came on 13th May, 1961, when he entered the 1-mile race at the Glamorgan Championships in Bargoed. Having completed two years consistent training it was no surprise that he won his first ever race comfortably in a time of 4-32.6. In early June, he won the Port Talbot Youths 880-yds (2-10) and the 1-mile (4-48) but was disappointed to finish 3rd in the South Wales Switchgear Sports mile in 4-25. On 24th June, 1961, Dil competed in the Welsh 1-mile Championship at Maindy Stadium, Cardiff. He comfortably won his heat in 4-26.2 and in only his 6th race ever, he won the Welsh Mile Championship in a time of 4-21.6!

In a 3-way match with Neath Grammar School and Neath Training Centre, PTH fielded a weakened team and could only finish in 2nd place. There were wins in the junior section for David Hughes (880, mile), Ken Quick (220) and Terry Schneider (110yds hurdles). For the seniors, Clive Arnold won the mile.

On 29th July, Dil Robbins ran for Wales in a triangular match with Scotland and Ireland. Although finishing 6th in a high-class field, Dil posted a new pb of 4-16.1. This performance came to the notice of Sir David Evans-Bevan of Margam Park who kindly gave Dil free use of the park at any time for his training.

Dillwyn Robbins, Welsh 1-Mile Champion (4-21.6), 1961

At an inter-club XC meeting in November, PTH emerged comfortable winners of both junior and senior races. The tough course around Margam Mountain didn't deter the PT runners, David Hughes won the junior race and PTH occupied the first three places in the senior race. 1st - Jim O'Brien, 2nd – John O'Brien and 3rd – David Townsend.

In December, two PTH athletes were invited to join the Commonwealth Games possibles squad – Dil Robbins and 75yds hurdles champion, Isabel Barden who was still at Sandfields school.

1962

The year started with a notable team success for PTH. Almost 200 runners took part in the Nos Galan 4-mile race at Mountain Ash. PTH, led home by Jim O'Brien in 9th place, were the top Welsh team. David Hughes was 18th and John O'Brien 49th.

On 6th January, William Johnson of PTH was elected chairman of Glamorgan County AAA.

Jim O'Brien had to be content with 2nd place at the Glamorgan County XC Championships at Llandaff Fields, but was still selected for the Inter-Counties match. There was further disappointment for Jim when he lost his way in the Fforestfach road race and failed to finish. David Hughes had his sat nav switched on in the junior race and was the clear winner. PTH also won the Junior team trophy.

At the S. Wales XC League in Newbridge Fields, Jim made no mistake and ran away to an easy win. David Hughes won the youth's race. A week later David was unlucky to lose the verdict in a sprint finish with William Stitfall at the Welsh Youth's XC Championships in Carmarthen.

Alderman Llewellyn Heycock announced at the AGM of the Welsh AAA on 27th January at the Jersey Beach Hotel that a running track and stadium was to be built at Sandfields Comprehensive School. The estimated cost was £64,000.

Roath Harriers gained a one-point win over PTH in a XC match at Margam on 3rd February. The individual honours belonged to PTH though. Jim O'Brien was 1st and David Hughes 2nd.

Jim O'Brien's misfortunes seemed to be multiplying. He fell while leading the Welsh 6-mile XC Championships at Newbridge Fields. He returned to the race and plodded bravely on for a deserved 2nd place.

The PTH AGM took place on 27th July at Glanafan Grammar School. Giving his report, AEW said – 'I do so with pride, as this club came into being by overcoming obstacles and difficulties to supply a need for the youth of Port Talbot to participate in athletics. Port Talbot has a wonderful tradition in Welsh athletics and its youth deserves better facilities than are available at present. In fact, its best athletes travel at their own expense to Maindy Stadium and the training Centre at Merthyr Mawr for specialized coaching.' Albert Blayney, commenting on the secretary's report, said it was deplorable that Port Talbot was not conscious of the need of proper facilities for local athletes. The following officers were elected: - President – Lord Llewellyn Heycock, Chairman – Albert Sheppard, Secretary – AEW, Treasurer – George Hapgood.

It was noted in July 1962 that PT had three very fine young prospects. 17-year-old Terry Schneider held ten Welsh and schools' records over the hurdles. When asked about his training, he replied that he ran in his garden hurdling the washing line and a home-made wooden hurdle. 18-year-old David Hughes of Margam had proved himself a runner to be reckoned with over 880-yds, mile and XC. David held records in Welsh, YMCA and county championships. Powerful Fred Pridham at only 15 showed an amazing turn of speed over 100 yds. Fred had won many titles at county and Boy's Clubs meetings. He put his dazzling speed down to the home-made blocks he used for training.

The S. Wales T&F League was held at Waterton Cross. PTH completely dominated the 2-mile race with David Hughes 1st, Dil Robbins 2nd and Jim O'Brien 3rd. All three were given the same time in the closest of finishes!

On Saturday morning 15th September, it looked like a complete washout for the Cavalcade of Sport on the Aberavon Prom. The sun eventually got his hat on in time for the 4x2-mile relay. PTH fielded their strongest team of Jim and John O'Brien, David Hughes and Dil Robins and were runaway winners.

The same team competed in the semi-final of the Welsh Road Relay Series with the same result, which meant that PTH qualified for the final round. They continued their winning ways at the S. Wales League Road Relays at Waterton Cross where both junior and senior teams were victorious. PTH could only manage 3rd place, however, in the final of the road relay series held in Cardiff.

Jim O'Brien won the first three S. Wales XC League races at Singleton Park, Margam and Garngoch. He was ably supported by Dil Robbins, David Townsend, John O'Brien and David Hughes.

1963

Early in 1963 it was agreed that the Welsh Marathon Championship was to be run on a 3-lap course starting and finishing on the Aberavon Prom. PTH hoped to play a prominent part in this event as Albert O'Brien had come out of retirement to run with his three brothers. The O'Briens were also to team up for the 2-man Cardiff to Swansea 51.5-mile relay. The teams were – Dil Robbins & Jim; Len Tew & Albert with John & Aneurin forming the final pairing.

The gloomy, wet July conditions did nothing to dispel the excitement at Aberavon Beach when international star, Brian Kilby, set the World's second fastest marathon time of 2-14.43. Much to the delight of the local crowd, Jim O'Brien finished 5th in a new pb of 2-30.35. Dil Robbins and Len Tew finished 10th and 20th to give PTH the Welsh Marathon Team Championship

29 Sep 1962

While in training for the marathon, Dil, Jim and Len ran along the beach at Kenfig. They came to a part where the sand had been washed away by a recent storm and had left a layer of waterlogged peaty soil exposed. They removed their trainers and ran barefoot through this layer leaving a trail of footprints behind them. The sand returned soon after, but several years later, the peat was exposed again, revealing the footprints left by our champion marathon team. There was much discussion about these footprints and the 'experts' stated that they must have been made by early Britons, possibly Stone Age!

Jim O'Brien and Dil Robbins filled the first two places in the 2-mile race in the S. Wales T&F League at Newbridge Fields later in July. Dil won the 1-mile race at the League match in Llandarcy at the end of July.

A common event in Scandinavia but little seen in Britain is the Paarlauf. Swansea Harriers held this event at their track in Ashleigh Road in August 1963. It can take many different forms, but this one consisted of 2-man teams running alternate 220yds on the track to a total of ten miles. The formidable pairing of Jim O'Brien and Dil Robbins raced away from the rest of the field, lapping all of them, to win in 45-35. On the same track later in the month, Jim won the 3-mile race in the SWL in 15-48.

Against top-notch opposition, including Newport, Swansea and Carmarthen, PTH pulled out all the stops to win the Swansea Road Relay in September. The team consisted of Jim O'Brien, Dil Robbins, David Hughes and Len Tew.

The XC season started on 12th October with a SWL match at Newbridge Fields. Jim O'Brien was the clear winner and with David Hughes 3rd, Dil Robbins 5th and Len Tew 6th, PTH comfortably won the team event. PTH continued to dominate the next three league races with Jim the individual winner and PT winning the team race.

The AGM was held on Saturday 23rd November, 1963. AEW reported that T&F results were disappointingly mediocre mainly due to the lack of adequate facilities. He was pleased to note that the road and XC teams had fared exceedingly well. The meeting felt that the club was justified in having its own club blazer and vest badge. A sub-committee was elected to pursue this objective. The officers elected were: - President – Lord Llewellyn Heycock, Chairman – Albert Sheppard, Secretary – AEW, Treasurer – George Hapgood, Club Captain – Dil Robbins, Vice-Captain – Jim O'Brien.

The PTH road runners again turned up trumps when they competed in the Gower 10-mile multi-terrain race on the 28th December. Jim O'Brien made light of the tough terrain to win in 52-32. PTH won the team title with Dil Robbins 3rd (53-54), David Townsend 4th (54-11) and Len Tew 7th (56-02).

1st January, 1964   Queen's New Year Honours List, Awarded MBE – Arthur Ernest Williams MM, President, Welsh Amateur Athletic Association

What a brilliant way to start the New Year – a thoroughly deserved honour! The following item was published a few days later: - *'A well-known personality, Mr. Williams has been actively associated with athletics for a great number of years and has been a member of the Welsh AAA since 1921. A life Vice-President since 1951, he has been President of the association for five years. An Olympic grade international referee, he was awarded a Plaque of Honour for his services to athletics in 1952. Mr. Williams is also a member of the Empire Games Council for Wales and is Chairman of the South Wales XC and Athletic League. An official of the old Port Talbot YMCA Harriers for 27 years, he was instrumental in forming the Port Talbot Harriers club and has held the position of Secretary since 1961. He was awarded the Board of Trade long service medal to the Port Talbot Company of the Coast Rocket Life Saving Company. He was awarded the Boy Scouts Association Silver Cross for saving a life when he took part in a dramatic rescue when Margam Wharf was being dredged. Mr. Williams received a battlefield decoration in France in WW1 when he was awarded the Military Medal. A Trustee of Trinity Methodist Church, he is married with one daughter. His wife is Mrs. Iverna Williams, LAM.'*

It was business as usual for Jim O'Brien at the start of 1964. He won all the XC races he entered including the Glamorgan and YMCA Championships, was selected for the county, along with David Townsend, and also for the Welsh YMCA team.

The runners in a road race at Llandarcy in February had some unusual competition. As they raced along the Jersey Marine they had to negotiate a pram race going the other way! This had no effect on Jim O'Brien though. He won the race and, assisted by Dil Robbins (3rd) and Len Tew (4th), PTH won the team trophy. A 4th place in the Welsh XC Championships was enough for Jim to earn selection for Wales in the XC international in Dublin. At the end of

March with placings of Jim (1st), Len (2nd), Dil (4th) and David Townsend 5th, PTH won the S. Wales XC League and were presented with the 'Our Boys Challenge Shield'.

It was interesting to note the formation of the Welsh Industries AAA in March under the instigation of AEW. In July SCoW formed an athletics team and became affiliated to WAAA.

Jim O'Brien and Dil Robbins finished 2nd behind Hereford in a 2-man 52-mile relay race from Cardiff to Swansea. The pair changed places every mile and led until only half a mile from the finish when Collins of Hereford overtook Jim to finish in 4hr54.39, 23 seconds ahead of PTH 4hr55.02.

PTH were still able to win the Welsh Marathon team title for the second time at Aberavon Prom even without top runner Jim O'Brien. The team was Dil Robbins, Roy Anthony and Len Tew.

The first Miami Beach Trophy relay race was held on the Prom at Aberavon on 18th July, 1964. Jim O'Brien was missing again after having his tonsils removed. The team of Dil Robbins, Roy Anthony, Len Tew and David Townsend claimed 2nd place behind a strong Coventry Godiva team.

The Welsh Industries Championships at Talbot Green had a bumper turnout of 224 athletes. Dil Robbins won the mile and was 3rd in the 3-miles. Jim O'Brien, back in training, won the 2-mile steeplechase and was 2nd in the 3-miles. Fred Pridham won the 100yds and 220 in the junior section.

Despite Jim and Dil filling the first two places in the SWL XC race at Singleton Park in October, PTH could only finish 2nd behind Swansea University. The only competition Jim had was from a friendly Labrador who ran alongside him for the last half mile. Jim's sprint finish was too good for the dog though. He wandered off and found a suitable tree!

1965

1965 started with a letter of objection to PT Council by the Federation of Ratepayers objecting to the construction of a sports stadium at Sandfields. The estimated cost had escalated to £104,000 and paying back the loan over 30 years would raise the total cost to more than £300,000. In addition, the stadium would require manning and they argued that the facility would not bring in sufficient income to cover these costs.

AEW was re-elected as President of WAAA for the 7th time in January, 1965, setting an all-time record for this position.

The first ever Inter-works XC race was held at SCoW on 6th February, 1965. The first two places were filled by Jim and Dil. They couldn't repeat this feat at the SWL XC in Singleton Park a week later, but did manage 2nd and 3rd. Despite winning the last Fixture on home soil at Brombil, PTH finished 2nd to Swansea University at the end of the S Wales XC League season.

Jim O'Brien set off like a scalded cat in the Round the Factories road race at Bridgend 'and had parted from his teammates and competitors as if he hated them'. Jim won of course, with Dil Robbins 2nd giving PTH the team prize.

Dil Robbins easily won a 5 1/2-mile handicap race at Llandarcy starting from scratch and giving four minutes to the slowest runner. On 15th May, Dil was again on the winner's podium taking the title in the Glamorgan County 3-mile Championship in 14-31.6.

Two young members of PTH turned in excellent performances in the junior section of the Welsh Industries Championships on 14th August. Daniel Jideofo won the long jump 22ft 4 1/2ins (6.82m) and the high jump 5ft10ins (1.78m). Alan Barham was the winner of the 880, mile and 1.5-mile steeplechase.

In one of the most exciting British Marathons ever held, 23-year-old Bill Adcocks ran away from the field to win in the superb time of 2-16.50. This was a combined Welsh and British Championship starting and finishing on Aberavon Prom. Jim O'Brien was forced to drop out after 20 miles and Lynn Hughes (Newport, 2-26.46) was the first Welshman home.

Only six teams lined up for the Miami Beach Cup relay race on 11th September. Jim O'Brien anchored his team of Dil Robbins, Alan Barham and John O'Brien to a comfortable win. A much-changed team still produced the same result at Llandarcy a week later. The PTH team was Bill Perkins, Derek Moss, Alan Barham and Roy Anthony.

With Jim O'Brien missing from the first two SWL XC races PTH could only manage 3rd and 4th in the team placings. Jim returned to the fold with 1st place at Waterton Cross and with Dil 2nd, PTH emerged as winners. At Gnoll Park on the 20th November, 1965, Jim and Dil were 1st and 3rd to put PTH on top of the team table.

1966

PTH dominated the West Glamorgan XC Championships at Singleton Park on 8th January, 1966. So absolute was the domination that the leading four teammates just coasted across the finish line together! All were given the same time, but the judges decided this order – Alan Barham 1st, Jim O'Brien 2nd, Dil Robbins 3rd and Bill Perkins 4th. Needless to say, PTH won the team event.

At the Welsh AAA AGM in January AEW was elected President for an 8th consecutive term.

PTH were not so dominant at the next XC fixture in Singleton Park. Alan Barham was 2nd and Dil Robbins 5th to give PTH the team event. With Dil 2nd and Jim 3rd, PTH won the final fixture of the SW XC League and with it the Our Boys Trophy. Dil won the prize for 1st overall individual. Taking a break from PTH duties, Alan Barham won the first ever Welsh Industries XC Championships by a comfortable margin.

Keith Brown (25-07) and David Morgan (25-11) pulled off a 1-2 at the Llandarcy 5-mile road race in March, 1966.

As well as being assistant secretary of PTH, Derek Moss was the secretary of the SCoW athletics team. Derek and chairman, Wyndham Smith, were going all out to recruit new members for their team.

At the AGM in April, 1966, all officers were re-elected. Chairman – Albert Sheppard, Secretary – AEW, Treasurer – George Hapgood.

With a pb of 2-14 to his credit, Brian Kilby of Coventry Godiva was the favourite to win the Welsh Marathon starting and finishing on Aberavon Prom on 16th July. Kilby set off at a scorching pace, but with only two miles to go, blew up and had to drop out. This left the door open for John Newsome (Wakefield) to win in 2-30.19. Welsh Champion in 2-31.10 was Hedydd Davies (Thames Valley Harriers and Carmarthen). The PTH team of Keith Brown 12th

(2-50.54), David Morgan 13th and Dell Johnson 14th who were both given the same time of 2-54.54 won the Welsh Team Championship.

The first Harry Secombe Trophy meeting was held at the Swansea track on 30th July. Dil Robbins was the only PTH to compete, winning the mile in 4-26.6. Dil went on to win the 2-mile race at the Inter-works event a week later in 9-55.2. His winning streak continued with victory in the Llandarcy 5-mile road race in 25-16.

Paul Bright was included in the British Junior ranking list for 880yds with his time of 1-58.4 when winning the Welsh Schools title in August.

Derek Moss, running for the SCoW team, led the first leg of the Miami Beach Cup relay until the last few strides when Paul Bright just overtook him. The PTH 'B' team won the cup with the PTH 'A' team second.

Dil Robbins was in outstanding form in the Gower 10-mile race on 8th October. He ran away from the opposition to win with a new pb of 49-40. Jim was 3rd and Keith Brown 9th to give PTH the team prize.

The SWL XC season started with a win for PTH at Llandarcy. Dil and Jim tied for 1st place. The second fixture, also at Llandarcy, was something of a blood bath. Several runners were hit by a swinging gate. John O'Brien had to have stitches in a nasty head wound. Others strayed off course causing arguments with an irate farmer and all had to go through deep mud on many parts of the course. Yet, it was agreed by the runners that they'd all had a good time!

It was reported from down under that 50-year-old John Nash had filled 29th place in the New Zealand 10-mile Championship. John was PTs top runner when he left Wales in 1955.

Sometime during the year, a tentative start had been made on the construction of the running track on the Sandfields School playing fields at Seaway Parade.

James Boyle was awarded the title 'Athlete of the Year 1966' for his record junior javelin throw of 201ft 7ins (61.45m).

The very last race of 1966 finished in 1967. This was, of course, the Nos Galan midnight race. Dil Robbins was given the honour of carrying the Mayor of Cardiff's message to Mountain Ash, and then managed to finish 44th out of the field of 448 in the 4-mile race.

Jim O'Brien and Dil Robbins ran for the West Glam team in the Inter-Counties XC Championships at Leicester. As captain, Dil was pleased to be presented with the Joe Turner Trophy for the Most Improved Team. The following week Dil, running for SCoW, won the Welsh Industries XC Championships at Llandarcy.

1967

AEW commented in late January that he had seen someone working on the new athletics track at Seaway Parade and wondered if this venture would become reality sometime in 1967.

Jim O'Brien took 9th place in the Welsh XC Championships in Barry at the end of February which earned him a place in the Welsh team for the international event two weeks later.

Running off scratch, 5½ minutes after the first man, Dil Robbins comfortably won the Llandarcy handicap race in mid-April.

The Glamorgan 3-mile Championship became a two-horse race with Dil Robbins setting the pace closely followed by Paul Darney (Birchgrove). Dil was the stronger on the final lap and surged away to win yet another county title. An equally brilliant performance from Shirley Ellis won her the 880yds title. John Davies (yes – author!) was a comfortable winner of the junior men's 880yds. All three were selected for the Glamorgan County team.

Dil repeated his 3-mile success in the West Glam Championships at Swansea with a winning time of 14-23.0. Paul Bright set the pace and won the 880 in the outstanding time of 1-56.3. Paul bettered this the following week by winning the Glamorgan Schools in 1-55.8.

Several PTH members turned out for the SCoW team in an Inter-works match at Llandarcy in July. For the senior team there were wins for Jim O'Brien (2-miles), Paul Bright (880) and for the juniors John Phillips (discus) and John Davies (880).

PTH sent a small team to compete in the Maesteg RFC sports in mid-July, Jim O'Brien won the 5-mile road race as expected. He then took part in the 880yds in the stadium. Nothing startling about that you might say. But the finish was remarkable in that the judges could not split Jim, Derek Moss and Alan Roper (Neath) on the finish line, so it ended up as a three-way tie for first!

Also, in July the Port Talbot District Youth Sports took place at the playing fields in Seaway Parade. The track was still far from finished which prompted AEW to exclaim, 'When are we going to have that track!'

Dil Robbins was forced to pull out all the stops in the 1-mile race at the Harry Secombe Trophy meeting in Swansea. He was pushed all the way by Roger Clarke of Bristol, but was victorious in 4-17.8.

At the Sennibridge sports. Jim O'Brien won the 5-mile road race and Derek Moss was the clear winner (this time!) of the 880 in 2-07.4.

It's been mostly about the men so far, but it's pleasing to report that the PTH ladies won the 4x110yds relay at the Swansea sports in early August. The team consisted of Janice O'Brien, Gillian Pitman, Dorothy Allen and Gaynor Blackwell. The whole team went on to represent West Glam in the Inter-Counties Championships.

Ladies to the fore again. At the Bridgend Road Races in November, the team of Margaret Lewis, Gaynor and Katrina Blackwell and Dorothy Allen comfortably won the team event.

We end 1967 with the sad news that D. J. P. Richards passed away in August at the age of 68. DJP was a founder member of PTYMCA Harriers in October, 1921. He first came to prominence as an athlete when he won the Welsh Novices XC Championship at Margam in 1922. Work took him to Newport where he went on to win 23 Welsh titles on the track, XC and walking.

1968

Track news – in January, 1968 it was revealed that the firm building the running track had gone into liquidation. The track had cost £60,000 at this stage, but during wet weather was like a sponge full of water. AEW commented that the track absorbed water from the surrounding land which was at a higher level. A council spokesman replied that additional drainage would be put in and the track would be ready for use in the Spring.

On a beautiful March day, Jim O'Brien and Dil Robbins claimed the first two places in the Round the Factories Road Race at Bridgend and PTH were team winners.

Jim O'Brien won two races in one at the Gnoll on 15th March in a combined SWL and YMCA XC Championships race. He was aptly awarded the Isaac O'Brien Cup for the YMCA race, but PTH could only manage 2nd place in SWL final table.

AEW was re-elected President of the WAAA for the 10th successive year at the AGM in Brecon. He was also presented with the Meritorious Plaque of the Welsh Industries Sports Council.

Dil Robbins and Jim O'Brien were joint winners of the West Glam XC Championships at Swansea Bay. Dil also won the Welsh Industries XC Championship at Margam a week later.

Two promising young PTH ladies, Gaynor Blackwell and Dorothy Allen attended a WAAA coaching course at Cardiff University in Llanrhymney on 18th & 19th April, 1968.

A meeting of the Welsh Counties representatives was held at Port Talbot where it was decided to roll out the new AAA 5-star award scheme throughout Wales.

The first of seven T&F meetings planned for Llandarcy took place on 25th May. Star of the meeting was Gaynor Blackwell who won the 80yds hurdles, 100 and long jump and was also 2nd in the discus and 880. Dorothy Allen also did well for 2nd in the 80ydsH, 100 and long jump.

On 20th June, AEW stated that, 'Things are looking very much brighter on the athletics front in Port Talbot, as the athletics track laid down so long ago has now come into use for schools and youth clubs. When, after teething troubles, this track settles down, it is going to be a boon to our athletes and the elimination of a host of headaches for local athletics clubs officials, who have long waited for this public amenity'.

Gaynor Blackwell won the Glamorgan Schools 80ydsH championship and ran for Glamorgan in the Schools Inter-County match. At the Welsh Games Gaynor was on top form to win the hurdles race in the splendid time of 11.0 seconds. At the Glamorgan County Championships Gaynor excelled once again winning the hurdles and the 100yds. Not to be outdone, Dorothy Allen won the Jong jump and was 2nd in the 100. As a result of their prowess, Gaynor and Dorothy were awarded 5-star certificates by the AAA.

British Steel (SCoW) dominated the Welsh Industries Championships at Barry on 24th August. As expected, Dil Robbins won the mile and 3-mile events.

There was good news and bad news at the end of 1968. The good news was for Swansea Harriers. The bad news was for PTH. Dil Robbins had resigned from PTH and joined Swansea Harriers. Dil considered himself primarily as a track runner over the middle-distance events. He became unsettled at PTH because of a lack of these events and felt he could only get the competition he desired at Swansea. It was a difficult and sad decision to make, but he felt that it was the only way forward for him. He didn't take the decision lightly because in those days you had to run as an individual with no club for nine months after resigning before you could appear in your new club's strip.

Here's a doggy story to end 1968. When Keith Brown set off at the start of the SWL XC at Newbridge Fields, his little Welsh sheepdog, Shoni, joined in the fun. Shoni disappeared at one stage, but only to take a quick drink from the River Ogmore. Thirst quenched, he sprinted to catch up with Keith and stayed with him to the finish. That great pace-making by Shoni pulled Keith through to 3rd place!

The Sandfields Comprehensive School gym was being used at this time on Mondays and Thursdays for winter training. The mixed bag of athletes who turned up were put through their paces with great enthusiasm by coach Terry Pugh.

Shoni was becoming a familiar sight at XC races, but even with his encouragement, PTH could only finish 3rd in the team table at the end of the SWL XC season.

The ladies of PTH had done rather well in 1968. Gaynor Blackwell and Dorothy Allen were both in the Welsh top ten for their events. Shirley Ellis was also in the list and along with her prowess as a tennis and hockey player was awarded the BBC Welsh Junior Girl Athlete of the Year.

1969

It was a day of joy on May 3rd, 1969 when Lord Heycock fired the pistol to start the first race of the West Glamorgan Championships on the new track at Seaway Parade. It was the first time in the 48-year history of PTH that a championship T&F event, had been held on a proper track in the town.

Fifteen members of PTH enjoyed a weekend trip to the Merthyr Mawr Training Centre in May 1969. It wasn't all fun and games though. They helped with the chores as well as taking part in the strenuous training sessions – and had to pay for the privilege into the bargain!

The first in a series of Junior matches in the West Glam Junior League was held at the Sandfields track on 24th May. There were wins in their age groups for Gaynor Blackwell (100m, 200m, discus), Katrina Blackwell (800m), Brian Cole (200m), Dorothy Allen (Long Jump), Peter Hughes (triple jump) and PTH finished 2nd in the team table to Swansea.

note that from 1969 onwards the metric system was adopted by GB to fall in line with the rest of Europe.

PTH juniors also did well at the Glamorgan Championships. Gaynor Blackwell won the 80mH and 100m. She also anchored the PTH team of Dorothy Allen, Gillian Pitman and Janice O'Brien to a win in the Intermediate girl's 4x100m relay. The team of Annette Thomas, Maria Kissack, Gina Proietti and Barbara Cove also won the junior women's 4x100m relay.

In the final match of the Welsh Athletics League at Jenner Park, Barry, Jim O'Brien scored a double when he won both the 3Km steeplechase and the 5km races.

The weather was perfect for the 6th Welsh Industries Championships and Dil Robbins made the most of it by winning the 1500m and 5Km. The improving Derek Moss ran well for 3rd place in the 1500m. Dil was awarded the athlete of the day Mettoy Trophy for his efforts.

Jim O'Brien, (58) star of track, road and cross-country

PTH gave their all in the last West Glam Junior League on their home track at Sandfields, but had to be content with 2nd place in the final team table.

Three members of PTH made a profitable journey to the Afon Taf track for a late season meeting. Jim O'Brien won the 5Km in 15-12.4, David Hughes the 1500m in 4-05.4 and Derek Moss was a close second in a pb of 4-06.0.

The AGM was held on 24th September, 1969. Officers elected were Patron – Lord Heycock, President – AEW, Chairman – Derek Moss, Secretary – J. W. L. Allen, Treasurer – George Hapgood, Chief Coach – Terry Pugh, Men's Captain – Jim O'Brien, Ladies Captain – Gaynor Blackwell.

In October, AEW was elected for an 11th term as President of the WAAA.

The XC season started with wins for Jim O'Brien and Gaynor Blackwell at Newbridge Fields. Both men's and ladies' teams topped the league tables.

Gaynor Blackwell was in superb form at the Cosford indoor meeting in December. She recorded wins in the 60m and a UK age group record in the 60mH. Also, in excellent form, Derek Moss won the 1Km race in a pb of 2-41.1.

1970s

What was planned to be an annual race was first held in January 1970, from the Sandfields Youth Centre. It was a frosty, lung-bursting evening when the runners set off and the usual suspects were soon out in front. Dil Robbins won the 4-mile race in 19-45, Jim O'Brien 2nd and Derek Moss 3rd.

Gaynor Blackwell appeared three times in the UK top ten ranking list for 80mH. Her times were 11.7 - 4th, 11.8 – 5th, 11.9 – 10th. Katrina Blackwell spread-eagled the field to coast home first in the Glamorgan Schools XC Championships in February. Two weeks later Katrina won her age group in the Welsh Ladies' XC Championships at Cwmbran. The sisters distinguished themselves at the Glamorgan Schools T&F Championships at Maindy Stadium in May. Gaynor won the 80mH and Katrina the 800m. At the same meeting Annette Thomas won the 175mH.

The Glamorgan County Championships were held at Jenner Park where the junior ladies team of Annette Thomas, Lorraine Thomas, Lynette Thomas and Jacqueline Jones won the 4x100m relay. Annette also won the 75mH and Pamela Osborne the high Jump. For the lads, Michael Hamilton won the Youth's high jump and Derek Moss the 1500m. PTH went on to win the first fixture of the West Glam Junior League at Maesteg in early July.

Gaynor Blackwell set a new record of 11.6 when she won the Welsh Schools 80mH Championship. Keeping it in the family, Katrina set a new record in winning the 800m in 2-23.2 beating the old record by more than 7 seconds!

The senior men took a team of only seven to the Welsh League division 2 fixture at Barry. Their plan to cover as many events as possible was successful as PTH topped the table at the end of the day. Derek Moss won the 1500m and 400mH while all credit to Mike Jenkins who covered twelve events! They went on to win promotion to Division 1 at the end of the season.

PTH hosted the second West Glam Junior League match at Sandfields and even without their star performers won the match comfortably. Several of the youngsters were in the Glamorgan team for the Inter-Counties match at the Sandfields track in early September. Despite wins by the Blackwell sisters, Annette Thomas and Chris Major, Glamorgan could only finish 2nd. Although the new track was in regular use by this time, the promised stand and changing rooms had not yet materialized.

AEW was elected President of WAAA for the 12th successive time at their AGM in October. Jim O'Brien was awarded a Meritorious Service Plaque and Terry Pugh was elected to the WAAA coaching committee.

The ever-improving Derek Moss recorded a pb of 4-23 in the mile event at the Nos Galan races and also ran in the 4-mile race finishing just a few seconds behind Jim O'Brien who was 32nd in a high-class field.

1971

In February, 1971, PTH were pleased to announce that the Welsh Marathon Championships were to return to Port Talbot. This time the Welsh 10-mile Race-walk Championship would be included as well.

PTH senior men were finding life difficult in Division 1 of the Welsh League. In the first meeting at Swansea in May they failed to record a single win and finished 5th in the table. The juniors were finding it almost as difficult in the West Glam League, but did manage wins from Annette Thomas and the relay team.

Gaynor Blackwell won double gold at the Welsh Schools Championships in Haverfordwest on 10th July. She was 1st in the long jump (5.14m) and the 100mH (16.5).

AEW lamented the fact that, after only one season, PTH senior men were relegated from division 1 of the Welsh League, 'The club has suffered grievously over the last few years through the desertion from its membership of those who one had hoped would have developed a sense of loyalty to their town and club'.

Bernard Plain (Cardiff) took more than five minutes off the record in the Welsh Marathon Championship at Aberavon with a time of 2-20.59. There were no finishers from PTH, but the organization of the event was deemed a great success.

The last match of the West Glam Junior League was held at Swansea at the end of August. Katrina Blackwell was absent on duty with the Welsh team and won her 800m race in the international match. PTH finished 3rd on the day and 2nd in the final league table.

The Welsh XC Association met at the Sandfields Youth Centre on October 15th, 1971, for a very special reason. On that date in 1921 a meeting was held in the old YMCA building at which the Harriers club was formed. One of the people present was AEW and it was to celebrate both his long association with athletics and the club's birthday 50 years before that the XC Association held its meeting in Port Talbot. AEW marked the occasion by presenting a president's chain of office to the association with these words, 'With so many other countries entering athletics. It is nice to think that this chain will be worn on many international occasions.' Also in October, AEW was elected for a 13th term as President of the WAAA.

1972

There was a general lack of information for 1972. A brief report in February indicated PTH had fallen on poor times. A SWL XC match took place in Llandarcy where the club was placed 5th in the team table.

In April, Katrina Blackwell and John Mescall appeared in Swansea colours at the Welsh Road Relay Championships.

It was announced in May that AEW had been nominated for the Award of Honour. This is the WAAA's most prestigious award for services to Welsh Athletics.

Two promising youngsters competed for their schools in the Welsh Youths Championships at Swansea in June. Michael Cole released a devastating final burst to win the 800m and Jeff Griffiths just edged ahead in a close-run final of the 400m.

Port Talbot's good name for organization lived up to its reputation when the Welsh Marathon Championship was once again held at Aberavon. Hedydd Davies (Sale and Carmarthen) won his 4th title in a time of 2-27.06. Little Len Tew was 15th.

AEW, at 80-years-old was presented with the WAAA Award of Honour by the Marquis of Exeter in November. Replying to the Marquis, AEW said that athletics was one of his absorbing interests and he still ran in XC events until he was nearly fifty. He also added that his one claim to fame in this field was that he was 'Welsh Champion Whipper-in' – or the last man home in every race!

A lifetime in sport is justly rewarded

A LIFETIME of devoted and outstanding service to athletics by Mr. Arthur Williams, the 80-year-old president of the Welsh Amateur Athletic Association, was recognised at the annual general meeting of the Amateur Athletic Association, in London, when he was presented with the Association's Award of Honour, a plaque in silver and gold on an ebony background.

The presentation was made by the Marquis of Exeter, president of the A.A.A. and an Olympic gold medallist in 1932, who offered his congratulations and paid glowing tribute to Mr. Williams and praised his great work in the promotion and development of athletics.

Mr. Williams suitably responded to this and other tributes paid him and presented the Marquis with a cheque for £300, which represented the fourth contribution of the total of £1,300 raised in Wales for the A.A.A.'s. Munich Olympics Appeal, which easily surpassed the target of £500.

A native of Bristol Mr. Williams, who lives at 13 Hafod Street, Port Talbot, came to Port Talbot as a young man in 1913 and immediately entered into various local activities.

Athletics was one of his absorbing interests and he participated in cross-country running until he was 50 years old. His one claim to fame

MR. ARTHUR WILLIAMS, M.B.E., president of the Welsh A.A.A., pictured with the A.A.A.'s Award of Honour which he has received in recognition of his outstanding service to athletics.

1973

It was difficult to find any information from 1973, but the earliest report was not good news. PTH couldn't raise a team for the last SWL XC race of the season and didn't feature in the top three in the final table.

PTH had the honour of staging the Welsh Road Relay Championships in April using the Sandfields Youth Centre as the base. There were more than 250 entrants who raced around the Sandfields streets, and although PTH didn't figure in the medals, the club was highly praised for their organization.

More bad news followed. The senior men couldn't raise a team for the first Welsh League fixture and were forced to drop out.

In the first Minor League meeting at Llandarcy on 16th June, there was some good running from the PTH youngsters including a win for 10-year-old Shaun Whelan in the 80m. The final league meeting took place in August, Swansea topping the table and PTH finishing 4th.

1974

1974 was another barren year for information about PTH. The club's only mention was a XC article in November. Michelle Morris and Sharon O'Brien made the West Glam team for the Inter-Counties XC Championships. Jim O'Brien was 4th and John Roberts 9th in the SWL XC at Singleton Park.

This article appeared in the Athletics Weekly of 12th January, 1974 –

With the passing of Bert Blayney at the age of 57, a link has been severed in the list of those Welsh athletes who left Wales to find athletic fame in England. He won the Welsh Novices Cross Country and ran well for Penrhys Harriers in the Rhondda. In London, he ran for Mitcham. It was as a marathon runner that Bert really shone and in the post war years he came back to run in the Welsh Marathon Champs as a member of Ealing Harriers (3rd in 1958). He came back to live in Wales and lived in Port Talbot, employed as a staff official in the famous Abbey Steelworks. Bert joined PTYMCA and then PTH in 1961. He took charge of all the marathon races that were so successfully organized by PTH among which was the one when a world record was missed by seconds by Brian Kilby.

1975

This article written by AEW appeared in the Guardian on 4th July, 1975, 'It is a long time since we were able to take pen and record the doings of Port Talbot Harriers, so it is a pleasure to report that after being in the doldrums, the club contemplates a new lease of life. The senior athletes either retired, or sought new clubs (probably the biggest loss to PTH was Jim O'Brien who had transferred to Bridgend because of the demise of the senior section), and only one club official stayed on to keep things going. There was always a large number of juniors, and it felt it was necessary to keep the tradition of athletics alive in Port Talbot, and to encourage these youngsters, that a meeting was called to form a new committee to take charge. The new officers were: - Chairman – W. Allen, Secretary – John Davies (not me!), Treasurer – Randall Lewis, Team Managers – Mrs. Peter Thomas and Annette Thomas.

The first Junior T&F League took place on 26th July at Brecon. The PTH youngsters battled bravely to win the team event. Special mention for sisters Julie and Clare Tayler, Pamela Walker, Tim O'Leary, and Graham Davies who all claimed maximum points.

In a T&F match with Brecon at Sandfields at the end of August the PTH team ran out winners again. On top form were the Tayler twins, Tim O'Leary and Huw Griffiths.

PTH fielded a weakened team for the last Junior League match at Barry on 19th September. Among those who stood out were Daniel Walker, Tim O'Leary, Nigel Davies and Mike Routliffe. PTH finished midway in the final table, but had the winter to prepare under new Chairman, Bernard O'Leary.

This article appeared in Athletics Weekly of 27th September, 1975 –

The sad death occurred recently of 75-year-old Will Owen, one of the founder members of Port Talbot YMCA Harriers. He won the Welsh Championship 100 yards in 1922 and 1923. The president of the Welsh AAA, 83-year-old Arthur Williams, recently took on the secretaryship of his club, PTH, as there was no one else to fill the breach following the resignation of the existing secretary. Arthur recently obtained a lorry-load of Dunlopillo for the high jump and pole vault landing areas at the Seaway Parade track. Port Talbot Harriers, thanks no doubt to the example set by the Welsh AAA President, now have a new secretary – J. Davies, Rowan Croft, 12b Richley Close, Baglan, Port Talbot.

On Saturday 18th October, 1975, AEW was elected as President of the WAAA for the 18th successive year.

It was a record turnout for the first Gwent XC League match of the season at a swampy Singleton Park in October. PTH were not only swamped by the conditions, but by the opposition as well. Chris Corish, Leigh Francis and Michelle Morris tried their best though. The second Gwent race was held at Newbridge Fields in November. PTH showed some improvement through Shaun Whelan, Chris Corish, Helen Francis and Clare Tayler.

Seven of our ladies were selected to represent West Glam at the Inter-Counties XC Championships at Brecon in November – Helen Francis, Pamela Walker, Susan James, Claire Tayler, Belinda Paisley, Geraldine Harris and Michelle Morris.

AEW was pleased to say that he'd had a Christmas card from John Nash who emigrated to Wellington, New Zealand in 1955. John was still going strong and wished to be remembered to all at PTH – and a Merry Christmas to you too John!

1976

The AGM was held in February, 1976. Chairman, Bernard O'Leary reported that membership had grown out of all expectation over the last year. Amongst the awards, Shaun Whelan was voted the Most Promising Athlete of the Year. Officials elected were: - Patron – Lord Heycock, President – AEW, Chairman – Bernard O'Leary, Secretary – John Davies (still not me!), Treasurer – Randall Lewis, Team Managers – Mrs. Maria Thomas, Derek Tayler, Glan Francis, Committee – Linda Harris, Ron Jones, Glan Phillips.

Four members of PTH ran for Glamorgan in the Youth Clubs XC County Championships at Llanidloes in March – Helen Francis, Michelle Morris, Belinda Paisley and Geraldine Harris.

PTH, with parents and officials supporting, took 41 athletes to the final Gwent XC race in Pontypool in March. They all struggled valiantly over the mud and hills, none more so than Wyn Allen who claimed 7th place in his age group only ten seconds behind the winner.

Only five members competed at the Swansea T&F meeting in April, but all recorded wins in their events. Helen Francis 800m (2-44.6), Graham Davies 400mH (57.0), Michelle Morris 1500m (6-05.0), Belinda Paisley 200m (30.0) and David Morgan 200m (23.4).

The first Junior League of the season was at Maindy Stadium where Geraldine Harris won the shot and long jump. Following swiftly on, the West Glam T&F Championships were held at Swansea with the following winners – Pamela Walker - high jump, 200m; Clare Tayler – 800m; Nigel Davies – 100 & 200m; Graham Davies – 100mH; David Morgan – 100 & 200m.

At the second Junior meeting, PTH clocked up 18 wins and 13 2nds. Shaun Whelan stood out with three wins – 200m, 800m and long jump.

The Glamorgan Youth Clubs Championships were held at Sandfields on 19th June. Sandfields Youth Club recorded 37 wins. The highlight, however, was Peter Williams' (Cymmer) commanding victory in the 1500m.

John Davies stood down as Secretary and Derek Tayler was the willing replacement.

David Morgan won a place in the Welsh Junior team for the international match in Edinburgh after convincing wins in the Welsh Youths and Schools Championships. In August, Pamela Walker was selected for Wales in a 3-way match with Scotland and Eire in Aberdeen She won the 200m (27.7) and the high jump (1.48m).

PTH finished 4th in the Glam Youth League at Swansea. Wins were recorded by Pamela Walker, Helen Francis, David Morgan, Shaun Whelan, Mike Reynolds and congratulations to Julie Tayler on setting a new league record in the javelin.

The seniors returned to Division-3 of the Welsh League with some style on 21st August. There were wins for David Morgan (100 & 200), Mike Routliffe (400) and Graham Davies (400mH). Others worthy of a mention were Leigh Francis, Aneurin O'Brien and Alan Furnell.

The last of the Glam Youth matches took place on 18th August. PTH finished 5th on the day and 5th in the final table.

George Hapgood gave over 40 years of his life to athletics as a competitor and official. Sadly, he passed away in early summer 1976. It was proposed in September to raise funds for a trophy to commemorate this well-loved personality. The trophy would be awarded annually to the outstanding Athlete of the Season.

A group of PTH athletes travelled to St. Athan to try their hands at indoor athletics on 19th November. It turned out to be a successful venture with wins for Mike Routliffe (Youths 60m), David Morgan (Junior 60m) and Geraldine Harris (high jump). PTH pulled out all the stops when the team of David Morgan, Leigh Francis, Mike Routliffe and Graham Davies won a thrilling 4x250m relay against top clubs Cardiff and Newport.

RECORD BREAKER

Pamela Walker a pupil at Sandfields Comprehensive School, Port Talbot, who broke the high jump record in the West Glamorgan A.A.A., held recently at Swansea, with a jump of 5 feet 1¼ inches.

She will now go on to represent her county in the National Schools A.A.A. to be held at Cwmbran Stadium on July 2.

She will compete in the high jump, the 200 metre and the relay events.

In December, Helen Francis and Claire Tayler ran for West Glam in the Inter-Counties XC Championships. Also in December, a cabaret dance was held in honour of two of PTH's outstanding athletes. At this function framed photographs were presented to Pamela Walker and David Morgan who both represented Wales in 1976.

1977

1977 opened with the West Glam XC Championships on 15th January. No winners, but 2nd places for Cathryn Williams and Helen Francis. Others showing up well were Claire and Julie Tayler, Peter Williams and Alan Furnell.

It had been many a year since a member of PTH had won a XC race. This was put to rights by Cathryn Williams when she won the minor girl's race in the Gwent XC League at Blaise Castle in February. Brother, Peter was 22nd in the Youth's race. Cathryn continued her good form with a convincing win in the Welsh XC Championship at Singleton Park.

The AGM was held in May, 1977. AEW remarked that the previous year had been one of progress and success. The club had achieved eleven West Glam titles, a Welsh Youth champion and international honours. Officers elected were: - President – AEW, Chairman – Bernard O'Leary, Secretary – Derek Tayler, Treasurer – Randall Lewis.

The West Glam T&F Championships were held at the Sandfields track on 19th May. Mike Routliffe won the Youth's 100, 200 and high jump. Cathryn Williams took the 1500m while brother Peter, was 2nd in his 1500m. Leigh Francis won the junior javelin while Ron Jones and Derek Tayler were 1st and 2nd in the senior javelin.

The Welsh Women's T&F Championships at Cwmbran provided competition of a high standard with no less than twelve new records being set. It was to the credit of PTH then, that two members came away with Welsh titles. Pamela Walker won the high jump with a leap of 1.55m and Julie Tayler set a new record in the minor's javelin with a throw of 22.82m, beating the old record by more than 4m. This record stood for 12 years.

Paula Thomas won the Welsh Schools long jump with a record leap of 4.96m. This was the best by any junior in Wales and earned Paula selection for Wales U17s against Scotland, Eire and N. Ireland.

Graham Davies won both the Welsh and Welsh Schools 400mH championships which earned him a call-up for the Wales U20 match against Combined Services.

The women's section caused a minor sensation when they won the last fixture of the Welsh T&F League. This moved them up to 2nd place in the final table and automatic promotion to division 1 for the 1978 season. There were wins for Paula Thomas (100m, long jump), Alison Paisley (shot, discus and javelin), Belinda Paisley (400m, 800m) and Geraldine Harris (high jump, long jump).

In December, Julie Tayler was presented with the 'Most Promising Thrower' trophy by Welsh Women's AAA team captain, Averil Williams.

1978

On the 21st January, 1978, our junior women came up trumps at the West Glam XC Championships on a tough course at Penclawdd. They filled the first six places and easily won the team prize. Cathryn Williams 1st, Louise Copp 2nd, Paula Thomas 3rd, Elizabeth Williams 4th, Sharon O'Brien 5th, Donna Thomas 6th. The minor girls also won the team prize with Julie Thomas 1st, Sian Morris 5th, Claire Paisley 6th and Claire Tayler 7th.

The final race of the Gwent XC League was held at Singleton Park in March. Catherine Corish and Cathryn Williams had run consistently well throughout the season and were rewarded with trophies as Gwent League Individual Champions.

Brilliant running in the Welsh Schools Championships saw Cathryn Williams finish 1st, Louise Copp 2nd and Elizabeth Williams 6th for all to earn selection for Welsh Schools against England, Ireland and Scotland Schools.

Fresh up into division 2 of the Welsh Women's T&F League, PTH made an impressive start to finish 2nd behind Cardiff at Maindy Stadium in May. Paula Thomas scored a treble in 100m, 200m and long jump. Louise Copp won the 1500m, Julie Tayler the javelin and long jump and Belinda Paisley the 400m.

The West Glam T&F Championships turned into a goldmine for our PTH youngsters. Twenty titles were won including three for Paula Thomas, and two each for Geraldine Harris, Julie Tayler, Shaun Whelan, Vince Lewis and Tim O'Leary.

In the first Welsh Men's T&F match PTH had another great day to top the team table. There were wins for Graham Davies (110mH, 400mH, 400m), Peter Williams (1500m, 5Km) and PTH won both relay races.

PTH junior ladies brought back five titles from the Welsh Women's T&F Championships at Cwmbran in June. Pamela Walker set a new high jump record with her spring-heeled leap of 1.58m. Paula Thomas leaped length-ways to set a long jump record with 5.30m. Julie Tayler's throw of 28.72m won the javelin. Cathryn Williams set a new pb of 4-52.2 in the 1500m and Louise Copp ran away with the 800m in 2-24.7.

Pamela Walker achieved even greater heights when she won the Welsh Schools high jump with a pb and championship record of 1.60m. At the same meeting Shaun Whelan was in fine form to win the 800m.

PTH recorded a convincing win in division 3 of the Welsh League in Barry. Graham Davies had a field day with wins in the 110mH, 400mH, long jump and high jump. Peter Williams won the 800m and 1500m. Mike Routliffe sped to victories in the 100m, 200m, long jump and high jump. PTH went on to completely dominate the last league meeting, topping the table and gaining automatic promotion to division 2 for 1979.

Our junior ladies proved unbeatable in the Welsh Women's Road Relay Championships at Bridgend. Louise Copp went straight into a lead which the other team members, Elizabeth Williams, Claire Paisley and Cathryn Williams never relinquished. The whole team recorded sub-8-minute times, Louise being the fastest of the day with 7-13.

On a sadder note, Port Talbot lost one of its most popular sportsmen when Cyril Evans passed away in November, 1978. Cyril was Welsh pole vault champion in 1937 and 1938. He served in the RAF during WW2 and came back to win the championship once more in 1948. Cyril was a light-hearted, humorous and friendly individual and held in high regard as a sportsman. He was an ardent bowls player and a keen member of the Cymric Glee Society.

AT long last — and after 58 years of organised athletics in Port Talbot, a British Athletics Championship has come to our Borough.

After being associated with all the athletes of both sexes and all ages since October 1921. first with Port Talbot YMCA Harriers and it's successor Port Talbot Harriers and AC, the writer can claim the privilege of commenting on the success of young Julie Tayler.

In the Women's AAA Championships at the Crystal Palace, London, Julie won the Women's Junior Javelin with a 33-60 metre throw under very adverse throwing conditions.

This was far below her best of the season as in the Celtic Games on August 4, in Belfast, she threw the javelin 36-46 metres to win for Wales, and in the Welsh Schools AA Championships at Cwmbran last July, made a new schools junior record of 36.10 metres. In June in the Welsh Open championships, she had a season's best of 38.48 metres which gained her championship status.

Success

This young 14 year old athlete has set a pattern for future successes which can inspire other local athletes to achieve.

To be the first local athlete to win a British Athletic championship is a record for all time, and one which has given great satisfaction to her coach, Mr. Ron Jones, who specialises in teaching the techniques of javelin throwing.

Ron was no mean exponent of javelin throwing and has trophies to prove his successes and being a graded judge in field events.

Another junior member of Port Talbot Harriers in the person of Tim O'Leary has been successfil in javelin throwing competition.

At Llandeilo last week, Tim won the boys javelin throw with a 42-40 metres affort, which was infinitely better than that returned by the youth and junior age group competitors above him.

Tim is a good soccer player and a dogged runner and both he and Julie Tayler are a credit to their club.

● **Julie Tayler**

1979

In January, 1979, three PTH ladies appeared in the UK ranking lists for 1978. Paula Thomas was 5th in the 200m table with 25.2. Pamela Walker 20th with her 1.60m high jump and Julie Tayler's 30.26 javelin throw placed her at 24th.

At the presentation evening, Claire Paisley and Shaun Whelan were awarded the Female and Male Athlete of the Year trophies.

In February, 1979, Julie Tayler was selected to represent GB in the European Catholic Student Games in Tralee, Eire in April. Julie went on to win the javelin in that competition with a throw of over 36m.

PTH ladies made an impressive start on their first appearance in division 6 of the Midlands Women's League at Telford. There were wins for Julie Tayler (javelin, long jump), Clare Tayler (75mH, high jump), Pamela Walker (80mH, high jump), and Sian Morris (100m, 200m).

The senior men fielded an under-strength team in the first foray into division 2 of the Welsh League in June. Wins came from Shaun Whelan (400m 54.1) and Mark Tayler (triple jump 10.93m). Alan Furnell picked up useful points in the 800m and a pb of 17-45 in the 5Km.

Shaun Whelan established himself as an 800m runner of considerable promise when he won the Welsh Schools Championship in 1-58.7. Shaun went on to win the Welsh Youth title in an even swifter time of 1-56.26.

Six of our ladies also won titles at the Schools Championships. Julie Tayler set a new javelin record with 36.10m. Paula Thomas (400m, 56.9), Cathryn Williams (1500m, 4-47.9), Louise Copp (800m, 2-21.7) and Pamela Walker (high jump, 1.59m).

The ladies did exceedingly well to finish 2nd team at the Midlands Women's League in July considering they were missing their best athletes on international duty. Wins were recorded by Sian Morris (100&200m), Clare Thomas (800m), Clare Tayler (long jump) and Catherine Corish (1500m).

Star athletes at the GYA in Llandeilo at the end of July were Tim O'Leary (javelin), Pamela Walker (100, 200m, high jump), Helen Francis (400, 800m).

At Port Talbot Harriers' presentation evening recently, Clare Paisley and Shaun Whelan received the Club's male and female Athlete of the Year awards. Clare was a member of the Club's Welsh Junior Women's Road Relay Championship winning team, while Shaun is a double Welsh Junior Champion at 200 and 800 metres.

In August, BP Chemicals donated a high jump wear sheet to the club which met the approval of champion high jumper, Pamela Walker.

Our ladies did exceptionally well, despite international calls, to hold off the challenge of Stourport and win division 6 of the Midlands Women's League. The team pulled together and most athletes covered multiple events. Sian Morris won the 100m and 200m, Louise

Copp won the 1500m and was 2nd in the 800m and 3Km. Susan James won the 800m with newcomer Debra Crowley a close 2nd.

Catherine Williams, at the age of 16, ran for Wales U21 versus Ireland. Cathy recorded a stunning time over 3Km of 9-50.8, the first Welsh lady to break 10 minutes for 3Km.

At the end of the 1979 T&F season and 58 years of athletics in Port Talbot, a British Championship was brought home by a club member. Julie Tayler overcame the wet and windy conditions at Crystal Palace to win the British Junior Women's Javelin Championship with a throw of 33.60m. To be the first local athlete to win a British title is a record for all time and one which gave great satisfaction to javelin coach, Ron Jones.

Debra Crowley made an impressive start to her XC career by comfortably winning the minor girl's race in the Gwent League at Bishop Vaughn in Swansea. Catherine Corish was 3rd and brother Chris had his best ever placing when finishing 7th in the boy's race. Others doing well were Alan Furnell, Vince Lewis and newcomer Neill Golding.

By November, 1979, Debbie Crowley and Cath Corish had established a stranglehold on the girls XC scene. Debbie was 1st and Cathy 2nd in the Gwent XC at Blaise Castle. They then teamed up with Clare Phillips and Susan James to completely demolish the opposition and win the Welsh Women's Road Relay Championships at Bridgend.

The presentation evening was held in December, 1979 at St. Joseph's Parish Hall. AEW paid tribute to the sparkling array of young talent that PTH now possessed. Awards were made to Stephanie Jones – Best Female Field Athlete, Paula Thomas – Best Female Track Athlete, Tim O'Leary – Best Male Field Athlete, Shaun Whelan – Best Male Track Athlete, Julie Tayler – Female Athlete of the Year, Chris Corish – Male Athlete of the Year. In addition, framed photos were given to Shaun Whelan and Catherine Williams on gaining their Welsh international vests.

1980s

The first event of 1980 was a trip to sunny Barrybados for the Round the Island road races. Once again Debbie Crowley and Cath Corish dominated with Debbie winning in 9-51 and Cath only 12 seconds adrift. Karen Howells finishing 4th and Debbie Bevan 19th gave PTH the team trophy. In the other races Chris Corish was 2nd and John Chick 10th.

Returning to the course where she won her first Welsh title, and only five months after breaking her leg, Cath Williams completed a remarkable comeback by winning the Welsh Intermediate XC championships at Singleton Park. Louise Copp was 5th, Elizabeth Williams 10th and Helen Francis 15th gaining PTH second place in the team championship. In the Youth's race Chris Corish was 2nd and John Chick 7th.

Debbie Crowley completed a grand slam of victories in the last Gwent XC race at Singleton Park in March, which made her the individual champion as well. Cath Corish was 6th and Karen Howells 7th. Chris Corish was 6th in his race and runner-up in the individual championship.

Our ladies started the T&F season in fine form with a win in the Welsh Women's League at Llanelli. They then travelled to Birmingham for the Midlands League. Victories were registered by Louise Copp (800m), Clare Tayler (80mH), Pamela Walker (high jump), Julie Tayler (javelin), Cath Williams (3Km) and Paula Thomas (400m).

At home in the GYA League, Tim O'Leary won the javelin with 42.20m and other strong performances came from Debbie Bevan, Francesca Mali and Jonathan Price.

Sian Morris ran into really good form in the Welsh Intermediate Women's T&F Championships at Cwmbran in June. Speedy Sian sprinted to a double with 12.5 in the 100m and 25.9 in the 200m. She also helped the PTH team of Julie Tayler, Paula Thomas and Pam Walker to victory in the 4x100m relay in 51.7. Cath Williams won the senior 5Km Championship with 17-45.2.

Shaun Whelan and Julie Tayler were selected to represent the Catholic Schools of Britain in the European Students Athletic Championships in Milan.

PTH ladies travelled to Warley endeavouring to retain their place in division 5 of the Midlands League in July. Louise Copp and Cath Williams got maximum points in the 1500m as did Paula Thomas and Sian Morris in the 400m. Stephanie Jones won the javelin, Clare Tayler the 80mH and Pam Walker the high jump. The team of Sian Morris, Clare Tayler, Pam Walker and Paula Thomas set a new club record of 51.2 when comfortably winning the 4x100m relay.

PTH ladies finished 3rd in the last Welsh Women's League, but it was enough to give them the division 2 championship by one point from Barry. There were wins for Clare Tayler (400mH), Louise Copp (1500m), Debbie Crowley, (junior 800m), Sherry Morrison (senior 800m), Julie Tayler (javelin) and Sian Morris (400m).

Debbie Crowley picked up where she left off the previous season with her 6th consecutive win in the Gwent XC League at Newbridge Fields in October. The outstanding male performance came from Phillip Williams who finished 6th in the colts race.

A very wet Bridgend Industrial Estate was the venue for the Welsh Women's Road Relay Championships. The junior team of Deborah Brambley, Debbie Crowley, Beverly Morgan and Cath Corish took little notice of the weather and sailed home to a comfortable win. Helen Francis, Elizabeth Williams, Clare Paisley and Cath Williams claimed 2nd place in the senior race.

As expected, Debbie Crowley was first home in the junior race of the Gwent XC at Blaise Castle. This was her 7th consecutive victory. Others who showed up well were Cath Corish, Chris Corish and Graham Smout.

Cath Williams was in top form at the Mike Sully XC races in October. She led from the start and, despite going off course and losing the lead, came back strongly to win. Debbie Crowley was just pipped at the post in the junior race and had to be content with 2nd place. Debbie more than made up for this by continuing her run of success in the Gwent League at Barry in February, 1981.

1981

Three titles were won by PTH at the Welsh XC Championships at Heath Park, Cardiff in February, 1981. The winners were Cath Williams, Debbie Crowley and PTH won the U17 team trophy.

Beverly Morgan ran strongly in the Schools Championship and earned a call-up to the Welsh Schools team.

10 out of 10! Full marks for Debbie Crowley after winning her tenth consecutive Gwent XC race at Singleton Park in March. Two years undefeated and two consecutive individual championship. And to add icing on the cake, Debbie became the first Welsh girl for fifteen years to win the British Schools Junior Girls XC title.

PTH athletes were well to the fore at the West Glam T&F Championships in May at Morfa Stadium. County titles were won by Leigh Francis (javelin), Mike Routliffe (100m, 200m), Richard Lewis (400m), Alison Batt (100m), Sian Morris (200m), Angela Richards (high jump), Clare Paisley (800m), Clare Tayler (80mH), Julie Tayler (javelin), Cath Corish (1500m).

With only eight athletes in their team, PTH ladies till managed to qualify for the second round of the Guardian Royal Exchange Cup at Yoevil in May. The PTH cause was helped by wins from Sian Morris (100m, 200m) and Cath Williams (3Km).

Disappointing team results in the Welsh Women's League and GYA were brightened by some winning performances from Ian Parry, Graham Smout, Debbie Crowley, Sian Morris and Julie Tayler.

Sian Morris claimed a comfortable victory in the Welsh Schools 400m Championship in July, 1981. Sian went on to gain a full Welsh vest, and in the match against N. Ireland and Brittany won her 400m event in 56.0. Sian appeared in no less than six internationals at various levels during the season.

On 15th October, 1981, Port Talbot Harriers celebrated its Diamond Jubilee. AEW had this to say about this special occasion, 'Queen Victoria lived as Queen of Great Britain for 60 years and I distinctly remember the Diamond Jubilee celebrations way back in 1897 and my tiny part in it as the recipient of a juicy orange, a bag of sweets and a solid sixpence. I wrote in the Guardian some years ago that it is the duty of young people to look forward and the privilege of the older folk to look back and I am going to do just that. Why, you may well ask? Well, on October 15th the Port Talbot Harriers A.C. celebrated its Diamond Jubilee and I well remember that evening in the old hut opposite the Grand Hotel when members of the Sea

Rovers Troop of the Scouts Association in collaboration with a few dedicated athletes joined forces to form the Port Talbot YMCA Harriers. All of us can say of some special occasion, 'I was there,' and I can say just that as I was there and not by the wildest stretch of the imagination did I think I would be spared 60 years afterwards to see this memorable occasion – the Diamond Jubilee.'

PICTURED here are two young student athletes from St. Joseph's Comprehensive School, Port Talbot, who left this week for Milan, where they will represent the Catholic Schools of Britain in the European Catholic Students Athletic Championships. They are two of only three students from Wales to be selected to take part.

The young man is Sean Whelan, of 36 Rosewood Avenue, Baglan, and the young lady is Miss Julie Tayler, of 184 Western Avenue, Sandfields, Port Talbot.

Sean will compete in the 800 metres event. Currently he is the 100 and 300 metres and high jump champion of the Junior Catholic Schools of Britain. In 1978 Sean was the 400 metres Welsh Schools champion, and in 1978 and 1979 he was the 800 metres Welsh Schools champion.

Julie is only 15 years old and is the present British junior javelin champion, holding the Welsh records in both the minor and junior categories of javelin throwing.

Both are members of the Port Talbot Harriers Athletic Club, of which Julie's father is the secreyary. Their friends in athletics and at their school will join in wishing them every success in the Milan championships.

In summing up 1981, it was a season of individual success and international calls. This meant that the best athletes were not available for club duties on many occasions resulting in relegation from division 5 of the Midland Women's League, the Welsh Women's League and the Glamorgan Young Athletes League.

1982

What a start to 1982. PTH ladies made a clean sweep of the West Glam XC Championships at Singleton Park on 2nd January. Our county champions were Debbie and Julie Crowley and Cath Williams. John Radford was determined not to be left out and strode out strongly to win the Colts race. Debbie went on to win the Schools XC Championship in March.

At the presentation evening, ten-year-old Huw Evans was voted the Best Male Track Athlete for his speedy sprinting. Huw was also an accomplished javelin thrower.

Debbie and Julie Crowley continued their winning ways with victories in the Gwent XC League at Newbridge Fields in February. Debbie was unbeatable in the Gwent scoring her 15th consecutive victory in the March race, an un-paralleled sequence stretching over three years! The sisters were also presented with their AAA 5-star awards along with Debbie Morgan and Andrew David.

After being plagued by travel fatigue and illness Cath Williams bounced back to win the Barry Half Marathon in the superb time of 1-17.15.

Louise Copp moved up from her favourite 800m distance to try her hand at 5Km with instant success. Louise won the Welsh Championship 5Km in May with a time of 17-45.0, only eight seconds short of the championship record.

A spur-of-the-moment decision launched Helen Francis on to long-distance success. She went to watch the Neath Marathon, and with no specific training, entered at the last moment. Helen was delighted to finish as 2nd lady in 4-05.13.

Despite fielding an under-strength team, PTH came out on top of division 6 of the Midlands Women's League at Tamworth. There were age-group wins for Clare Tayler (100mH, 400mH), Julie Tayler (javelin), Bev Morgan (1500m), Claire Paisley (800m) and Ceri Brambley (1500m).

Andrew Millard set a new league record of 23.86m for the discus at the GYA in Haverfordwest. He also won the shot and 100m. Andrew David won the 100m, 400m and was 2nd in the 200m. Debbie Crowley won the 800m and Bev Morgan the 1500m.

At a T&F meeting in Cwmbran, Andrea Williams astonished everyone by winning the 400m in 61.2, the fastest time ever by a 13-year-old Welsh girl. At the same meeting Claire Paisley set a new pb of 4-37.0 when winning the 1500m.

At the Neath T&F meeting in July it was a tale of two sisters. Cath and Elizabeth Williams crossed the line together in the 3½mile road race. On the track, Ceri Brambley won the junior 1500m and sister Debra the intermediate 1500m.

Coach Doug Cole, took a willing team with him for the GYA in the Rhondda Valley. Prominent in the boy's events was Andrew David who achieved a hat-trick of wins in the 100m, 200m and 400m. Other boys to record wins were Andrew Millard, David Parfitt, and Gerald Walker. Wins by the girls came from Debbie and Julie Crowley, Karen Perrett, Bev Morgan and Andrea Williams.

In the last Welsh Women's League at Barry, PTH were relegated from division 2 by just one point. The team tried hard with wins from Pam Walker, Julie Tayler, Joanne Tayler and Julie Crowley.

PTH fared better the following week when they travelled to Tamworth for the Midlands Women's League. With four top athletes on international duty the team of ten managed to retain their place in division 6 with wins from Bev Morgan, Clare Tayler and Andrea Williams.

The younger athletes brushed off the disappointments experienced in other leagues by topping the table in the BP Young Athletes League. Outstanding as usual were Andrew Millard, Julie Crowley, Gerald Walker, Joanne Tayler and Ceri Brambley.

The first full British Athletics vest awarded to a local athlete was gained by Sian Morris of Cwmafan and Port Talbot Harriers. Since representing Wales for the first time in 1980, Sian had gone on to win an impressive total of 16 representative vests across various ages and associations.

Sian Morris, resplendent in her British vest.

Debbie Crowley continued her amazing run of success in the Gwent XC League with yet another win at Blaise Castle in October.

Louise Copp, still recovering from injury, was still able to record a time of 1-20.08 to win the Afan Half Marathon for the second successive year. In December, 1982, Louise made light work of the tough Vale of Neath 10-mile road race. Her time of 63.00 was good enough to give her first place in the ladies' race – and ahead of most of the men as well!

1983

In January of 1983, just before his 90th birthday, the indefatigable AEW was appointed chairman of the Welsh branch of the British Olympic Association.

'Happy Birthday Arthur!' That was the message from hundreds of well-wishers on the occasion of AEW's 90th birthday on the 22nd January 1983. Arthur's neighbours gathered together to give him a beautiful birthday cake decorated with the Olympic Rings. There was a surprise from his friends at PTH as well, when he was presented with a framed plaque with the inscription 'To A. E. Arthur Williams MBE MM, on the occasion of his 90th birthday 22nd January, 1983, from the Port Talbot Harriers and Athletic Club'

On Sunday 6th February, Louise Copp, with a time of 36.00, was the ladies winner in the first ever Cwmafan 10Km. Following fine wins in the Neath 5-mile, Vale of Neath 10-mile and the West Glam XC Championships, Louise was selected for the Welsh Women's XC team. Totally unawed by her first appearance in a Welsh vest, Louise romped to a convincing win. Two weeks later in the World XC Championships at Gateshead she finished well up the field and was second Welsh runner home after Cardiff's Kim Lock.

Having won the first three of the season's Gwent XC races, Debbie Crowley's magnificent run of eighteen consecutive victories sadly came to an end in February. On a course like sticky toffee at Newbridge Fields, Debbie lost a shoe not once, but twice. The distance she conceded proved too great to make up, even for the brilliant Debbie.

Elizabeth Williams seemed to have found a new dimension to her athletics when she completed the London Marathon. Liz was delighted with her time of 2-57, comfortably inside the magic 3-hour barrier.

An unusual and special event occurred in April when sisters Debbie and Julie Crowley both ran for Wales in the British Schools XC international in Bray, Ireland. It was 16-year-old Debbie's 11th vest and 11-year-old Julie's first. In super form and also gaining her first Welsh vest was 12-year-old, fleet-footed Lisa Carthew.

PTH consolidated their place in division 2 of the GYA League with a 3rd place finish at Haverfordwest in May. Maximum points were gained by Debbie and Julie Crowley, Ceri Brambley, Karen Derrett, Michelle Ansell, Andrea Stone, Andrew Millard, Mike Powell and Joanne Tayler.

June was a good month for PTH. It started with the juniors winning the Kate Williams Trophy on our own Sandfields track. Sian Morris ran the 400m for GB against Finland and produced a fine pb of 52.80 to win the race. A speedy 24.6 also won her the Welsh U20 200m title in Cwmbran. More Welsh Championship wins came from Andrea Williams (U17 400m, 60.4), Julie Tayler (U20 javelin, 34.76m), Debbie Crowley (U17 800m, 2-20.6), Lisa Carthew (U13 800m, 2-32.8) and Julie Crowley (U13 1500m, 5-11.1).

A strong performance from PTH saw the club move up to 3rd place in the GYA on the Rhondda track. Starring athletes were Derek Campbell, Andrew Millard, Gerald Walker, Andrea Williams, Dawn Stone and Lisa Carthew.

The Welsh Women's League was another happy hunting ground for PTH when the club topped division 3 at the end of the T&F season. There were good performances from Julie Tayler and Stephanie Jones in the javelin in a great team effort. PTH were sorry to lose the services of fine athlete Louise Copp when she transferred to Cardiff.

Now comes the moment I've been dreading while writing this history. The Grand Old Man of Sport, Arthur Ernest Williams, passed away on 2nd November, 1983 after a short illness. Much to my regret, I only met him on a few brief occasions, but having read his AEW reports in the guardian from the 1920s up to the 1980s, I feel I knew him well. The extract at the beginning of this book says it all and I don't feel I can add any more, except – Goodbye Arthur, and thank you for all the selfless work you did for Welsh Athletics and Port Talbot Harriers in particular.

Making a special athletic occasion, two Port Talbot sisters, Deborah and Julie Crowley recently competed for Wales in the same British Schools Cross Country International meeting in Bray, Ireland.

Deborah, 16-year-old, gained her 11th Welsh vest while, younger sister Julie, still only 11 years old, probably the youngest ever Welsh International, made her debut and gained her 1st Welsh vest.

Both are pupils of Glanafan Comprehensive School, Port Talbot and formerly of Sandfields Junior School, Port Talbot.

The presentation evening was held at St. Joseph's Hall on 16 December. Trophies were presented to Julie Crowley (Best Female Track Athlete), Mike Powell (Best Male Track Athlete), Audra Stone (Best Female Field Athlete), Andrew Millard (Best Male Field Athlete and Athlete of the Year), Debbie Crowley (Female XC Athlete of the Year), Alan Furnell (Male XC Athlete of the Year), Dawn Stone (Female Athlete of the Year) and Andrea Williams was presented with a framed photograph.

1984

Cold and icy conditions faced the runners for the second Cwmafan 10Km race on 15th January, 1984. That didn't deter Ceri Brambley though. She made light of the Arctic conditions with a time of 40-21 to win the ladies race.

During February, two of our young ladies figured prominently in XC races. Julie Crowley won both the Welsh and Schools Championships. Bev Morgan claimed two 2nd spots in these races.

The younger members of PTH collected four gold medals at the Welsh Indoor Championships at St. Athan in April. Andrew Millard won the shot with 10.65m, Joanne Tayler the high jump with 1.20m, Michelle Lloyd the 150m in 22.5 and Dawn Stone the 600m in 1-48.2.

With Jim O'Brien once again running for PTH, the senior men won three of the five West Glam XC races and the First Division title. Doug Johnston, David Richards, Alan Furnell and John Davies all played prominent parts in the success of the team.

10-year-old Louise Evans won a trophy for Pentathlon Personality of the Week at Barry, Butlins when she passed the Silver Standard of the Council for Physical Recreation with flying colours. She returned two weeks later and won the Gold Standard with equal ease.

There were some good results for the youngsters in the GYA at Carmarthen in June. Wins were recorded by Michelle Lloyd (100m, 200m), Julie Crowley (800m), Dawn Stone (200m) and Debra Fisher (200m).

The second GYA meeting was in Brecon where PTH finished 2nd in the team table. Prominent were Debbie Crowley, Julie Tayler, Michelle Lloyd and Karen Williams. High spot of the 3rd meeting was a tremendous treble for Karen Williams in the high jump, long jump and shot. Karen went on, in August, to win the Welsh U13 shot Championship with a throw of 7.21m and also won the pentathlon. Andrew Millard won the U15 200m Championship with 24.9. The team of Kerry Davies, Joanne Tayler, Karen Williams and Michelle Lloyd combined superbly to win gold in the U13 4x200m Welsh Championship.

Julie Crowley, only 13-years-old, was the first female home in the Afan Fun Run held on the Promenade on 6th October.

Louise Evans, by this time still only 11-years-old, won the Decathlete of the Year award sponsored by the Council for Physical Recreation. Along with this award went a £1000 sports scholarship to be used for coaching, equipment and travelling expenses.

The Welsh Schools XC Championships were held in November at Newtown. Showing a clean pair of heels to the opposition, Lisa Carthew won the Junior girls gold and Bev Morgan the senior girls.

With many of the stars missing, there was some solid running from the rest of the PTH team in all three of the Gwent XC races before the end of 1984. The burden rested mainly on Julie Crowley, Louise Evans, Bev Morgan, Gareth Edwards, Alan Perkins, John Davies and Ian Swanson.

The inaugural running of the A. E. Williams Road Relay took place on a sunny, late autumn day in 1984. Seventeen teams took part in this keenly contested event over a 4-mile course from Western Avenue to the Beach Hotel and back. Winners were Bridgend AC with their last leg runner, Ian Hamer, recording the fastest time of the day 19-51. The PTH team, who came second, included Dai Richards and Sean Whelan.

1985

In January 1985, PTH men's team recorded 2nd place in the 'round the res' race from BSC, Margam, led home by team captain, Dai Richards, who finished 4th.

At the annual presentation held in St. Joseph's Hall, the following awards were made – Best Female Athlete – Kerry Davies; Best Male Athlete – Andrew David; Best Female XC and Best Track Athlete – Julie Crowley; Best Male XC – John Davies.

In March 1985, representing West Glam at the Welsh Schools Inter-Counties Championships, Beverly Morgan won the Senior Girls race and Lisa Carthew won the Junior Girls race.

The club was fortunate to have seven coaches at this stage headed by Doug Griffiths (sprints) and Ron Jones (field).

March proved to be profitable for the men's team. After winning the last West Glam XC match, they went on to win the West Glam Road Relay. The winning team was Aaron Jones, Neill Golding, Dai Richards and Alan Perkins.

Dawn Stone had the distinction of becoming the first member of PTH to gain an award for completing 25 consecutive Gwent League XC races. This meant five years without missing a race.

In April, 1985 Julie Crowley scored a double. Firstly, she won the WAAA indoor 600m title at St. Athan in a time of 1-43.6. She followed this up with a win in the Ynys Park Junior Lady's Road Race over a 5K course.

Also in April, sisters Lisa and Laura Carthew represented Wales in the British Schools XC International. Lisa finished a creditable 5th and Laura 22nd.

Against strong opposition, the senior men finished 3rd in the Welsh T&F League at Morfa in May. There were wins for Dai Richards (steeplechase, 'B' javelin), Neill Golding (long jump) and Andrew Millard (100m).

The juniors were away in Haverfordwest for the Glamorgan Young Athletes League. There were strong performances from Louise Evans, Julie Crowley, Michelle Lloyd, Mike Powell, Andrew Millard and Andrew Langford.

Several new members turned out for PTH in the Kate Williams League at Western Avenue. Top of the tree was Stuart Robbins with wins at 70m, 100m and a league record in the long jump.

The WAAA Women's T&F Championships was a fitting occasion for PTH to wear their new club vests for the first time. The new colours consisted of narrow red and black diagonal stripes against the background of a white vest. The black vest with wide red chest hoop remained as the club's second colours.

It was a day of disappointment though with no titles being won and Julie Crowley having to drop out of the 800m final because of injury. There was better news for Michelle Lloyd, when she heard that she had been selected to represent Welsh Schools.

There was a hat-trick of wins for Mike Powell (100m, 110mH, long jump) in the Welsh League at Cwmbran. First-timer, Kevin Corcoran ran a controlled race to win the 5K. The following day, 30th June, the team of Kevin Corcoran, Alan Perkins, John Davies and Mike Kelleher packed well to win the Margam Park 5K XC race.

Non-stop rain forced the Kate Williams League organisers to abandon the meeting at Carmarthen in mid-afternoon. The weather did not deter Mike Kelleher, Michelle Lloyd, Sarah Lindsey and Julie Crowley who all recorded fine wins.

The senior men's team could only manage 3rd place in the final Welsh League at Morfa in August, failing narrowly to gain promotion to Div 3. The runners ran well, but it was mainly due to a lack of field eventers that promotion was missed.

Beverly Morgan was rated by her coach, Colin Daley, as one of the most promising athletes in Wales. She had represented her country at different age groups more than twenty times and was the current WAAA Women's XC champion.

The 1985 track season ended with a home fixture of the Kate Williams League. Outstanding were Stuart Robbins with a new league record of 3.65m in the long jump. Other winners were Robert Collins, Martin Hines, Michelle Lloyd, Melanie Williams and another superb league record for Julie Crowley when she won the 1500m in 5-01.

At the annual presentation evening pride of place went to Michelle Lloyd who represented Welsh Schools and was presented with a framed photograph. Alan Perkins and Gareth Edwards jointly won the Best Male XC trophy and Neill Golding was best male field athlete.

Sixteen teams took part in the AEW Road Relay in atrocious weather conditions on 1st December. The PTH team of John Davies, Alan Perkins, Mike Worlock and Dai Richards claimed 3rd place.

1986

The senior men's team struggled for form in the West Glam XC League. It wasn't until 9th

March, 1986 that they were able to field their strongest team. Some good packing meant that they won this last fixture and ended the season as runners-up to Swansea. Jim O'Brien, although still a member of Bridgend, gave his all as usual. He was well-supported by Dai Richards, Jeff Rees, Alan Perkins, Gareth Edwards and John Davies.

Also in March, superb running by Julie Crowley gave her an impressive win in the Welsh Schools XC Championships at Newtown. Julie had already run for Wales on three previous occasions and this win earned her selection for the schools team for the 4th time. Julie confirmed her status as number one junior ladies XC runner with comfortable wins in the Welsh Inter-Counties Championships and the WAAA XC Champs at Heath Park, Cardiff.

Jeff Rees set a new course record of 44-20 while winning the Taibach RFC 8-mile multi-terrain race on 4th May. The race was dominated by PTH with Kevin Corcoran 2nd (44-42), John Davies 7th (46-55), David Waters 8th (47-42). David Waters was also the 1st Taibach RFC member. Louise Evans was 2nd (21-10) in the separate ladies race.

The first Welsh Men's T&F League took place at Morfa Stadium on 10th May, 1986. Outstanding were Dai Richards (1st 'A' steeplechase), Alan Perkins (1st 'B' steeplechase), Andrew David (1st 'A' 100m) and Kevin Corcoran with a pb of 15-52 while winning the 5Km.

Although, having transferred to Cardiff AAC, Cwmafan girl Sian Morris, was delighted to have recorded a pb of 23.82 in the 200m at the Edinburgh Commonwealth Games. Sian was even more delighted to win a bronze medal as part of the record-breaking 4x100m relay team.

Andrew 'doubled' (Millard & David) gained double victories in the sprints to lead the way for PTH at the final Welsh League match in Cwmbran. Ably assisted throughout the four matches by Dai Richards, Alan Perkins, Kevin Corcoran and with staunch support in the field from Neill Golding and Andrew Langford, PTH men claimed 2nd place in division 3 and promotion to division 2.

Unfortunately, no information could be discovered about the Women's League, but our ladies also performed miracles with limited resources to gain promotion to division 1.

13-year-old Louise Evans won her second gold medal in the pentathlete scheme at Barry Island Butlins in July. The scheme was sponsored by the Council for Physical Recreation.

John Davies was the only Port Talbot Harrier who entered the Sports Council 3$1/4$ mile run in Margam Park on 16th August. In a close-run race his time of 19-33 was just good enough to give him 1st place.

Port Talbot runners featured prominently in the Cardiff Marathon on 7th September. Jeff Rees was 6th (2hrs35-34), John Davies 36th (2hrs55-50), Alan Perkins 77th (3hrs07-42) and Liz Williams 3rd lady (3hrs27-10). Jim O'Brien was 1st veteran (1hr12-50) in the half marathon race.

Very few Harriers turned out for the Afan Half Marathon and Fun Run on 26th October. Of those who did, Kyle Jones won the 3Km U11 race, Julie Crowley won the U15 and Dil Robbins was 1st veteran. In the half marathon, John Davies was 6th (1hr18-37) and Frances Gill was 3rd lady (1hr39-57).

PTH made an inauspicious start to the XC season. Results were moderate and star runner, Julie Crowley was injured. The only highlight was a win for Kyle Jones in the first Gwent XC Novices race in October.

The last event of 1986 was the AEW Road Relay on 12th December. The race was held in atrocious weather and the PTH team of Alan Perkins, Jeff Rees, Mike Worlock and John Davies could only manage 5th place.

1987

In March 1987 the XC season came to a close with hardly a highlight to mention. Novice, Kyle Jones, was the exception. He looked a runner of rare promise with 2nd place in the last two Gwent League races.

21-year-old Chris Corish won a gold medal as part of the Loughborough College team which finished 1st in the British Universities XC Championships. Chris also won the Clubman of the year award.

At the WAAA Indoor Championships in March the juniors had some success. Julie

Crowley won the 600m and there were 2nd spots for Kyle Jones (1Km) and Joanne Jones (60m, 150m).

There were several wins for PTH in the Glamorgan Young Athletes League, but the results in the West Glam T&F Championships were quite impressive. Wins were recorded by: - Joanne James (100m, 200m); Bethan Thomas (800m); Dawn Stone (100m, 200m, shot); Andrea Stone (discus); Andrew Millard (200m); Mike Kelleher (800m) and Kyle Jones (1500m).

Despite these encouraging championship victories PTH struggled for survival in all the T&F leagues during the summer of 1987. The ladies just managed to keep their places in the Midlands Women's and Welsh Leagues, as did the juniors in the GYA. The senior men failed in their battle. After just one season in division 2 of the Welsh League they were relegated back to division 3. There were several reasons for this, the main ones being a lack of field eventers and unavailability of athletes.

Now 14-years-old, Louise Evans won her 4th consecutive gold medal in the National Pentathlete Awards Scheme in August. Louise, by this time, was a member of Swansea Harriers.

Another high note of the year was the selection of Joanne Tayler to represent Welsh Schools in the 400m and the 4x400m relay.

The cross-country season started again in October with an improved turn out for the senior men. Although results were nothing to write home about, the men's team was boosted by the return of Aaron Jones from injury. Aaron turned in some pretty useful XC performances and was consistently the first PTH runner to finish. There were no XC reports to be found for the juniors and ladies I'm sorry to say.

1988

The year started well with the senior men winning the division 2 team race in the West Glam XC League at the BSC, Margam. Steve Wilkinson, making his debut for PTH, ran superbly for 10th place.

An interesting innovation was initiated by Kevin Corcoran and John Davies. The idea was a club championship for the senior men 'to promote a greater level of fitness, competition and communication' between the members. It consisted of a series of races ranging from 1500m to half marathon. The winner would be awarded 20 points, second 19 pts etc. There would be a trophy each for the men's winner and the over 40 winner at the end of the year. In order to help communication Kevin Corcoran suggested a newsletter should be issued at regular intervals (this was before the days of internet and Facebook remember!). The newsletter, written by John Davies, was titled Paperchase.

The men's team went on in March to consolidate their 2nd place in division 2 of the West Glam XC League winning promotion to division 1 for the 1988/89 season.

At the last Gwent XC race, Ian Swanson, Neill Golding and Dai (Ginger) Jones all received awards for completing 25 consecutive Gwent fixtures. Dai Ginger was a single man and his life was devoted to athletics. He was manager of both senior and junior teams and also a field judge. Dai was also something of a character. His favourite way of carbo-loading before a race was a Mars bar washed down with a pint of beer!

Also, in March the team of John Davies, Alan Perkins, Mike Worlock and Gareth Edwards claimed 2nd place in the West Glam Road Relay Champs at BP Llandarcy.

Joanne James set a new record for the 70m hurdles (12.2) at the GYA in Barry in May. Joanne also won the 200m and high jump. At the same meeting, colt Kyle Jones, set a new league record of 4-54.6 for the 1500m.

A depleted ladies team was grateful to avoid relegation and finished 4th in division 5 of the Midlands Womens League at Nottingham. Outstanding performers were Rachel Beynon, Clare O'Callaghan and Julie Bowen.

The youngsters also escaped relegation, finishing 4th in the GYA with a strong performance at Barry. The team was not without its problems. In a home match at Seaway Parade one of the boys (who shall remain nameless) was playing soccer on the nearby pitch. Without a regular long jumper, he was persuaded to come across to the track, take a jump and then return to the soccer match!

John Davies and Geoff Pugh finished 3rd and 4th veterans at the WGXC Champs and were selected to represent the county in December, 1988. Also selected for the senior men was Alan Furnell.

The new club championship was deemed a huge success by the men's section. Winner was Alan Perkins and Geoff Pugh was the over 40 champion. Alan Manning, the generous owner of Avlon Motors, donated the trophies to the winners.

1989

In 1989, PTH had no clubhouse. The juniors trained in the winter at Sandfields Comprehensive gym and the senior men met at the Afan Lido. The Seaway Parade track was the main venue for summer training.

The cross-country season didn't go well for the senior men. Even with Jim O'Brien back as second claim for the last West Glam at Tonna, PTH were relegated back to division 2 after only one year in division 1.

There were a number of successes at the West Glam T&F Championships at Morfa in May. In the youths age group, Andrew Davies scored a fine double with wins in the 400m (54.7) and the 800m (2-10.6). Ceri Stephens also claimed a double winning the minor girls 100m (13.9) and 200m (28.4). For the senior ladies, Clare O'Callaghan won the 400mH (73.6) and Suzanne Edwards the 1500m (5-49.2). Ceri Stephens went on to win the sprint double with times of 13.5 and 27.5 at the Welsh Junior Champs in June.

Vince Lewis produced a fine all-round performance to win the BP Baglan Bay Septathlon at Seaway Parade, also in June.

During the summer of 1989, Gareth Edwards ran into exceptionally good form setting a Welsh League division 4 record of 10-03.9 for the 3K steeplechase.

During the summer of 1989, it was said, allegedly, that the current committee were fed up with acting as babysitters for parents who left their children with the Harriers at training sessions. In most cases, these youngsters did not compete for the club and the parents never offered to help. It was also suggested that enough was enough and PTH should be disbanded. The senior section held a meeting and decided to do their best to keep the club going. At the EGM in August the situation was discussed and it was decided that, because there was no one to manage the junior and lady's sections, they would close. Our top female runner, Frances Gill, was disappointed with the decision, but continued her athletic career with Neath Harriers. The club would then continue as a senior men's club only. Enquiries were made with Welsh Athletics as to whether this was possible. On 14th September another meeting voted 15-11 against the proposal to close the club completely. Secretary, Derek Tayler and chairman, Gwyn Stone stood down as did the rest of the general committee, except for Glan Millard who was re-elected as treasurer. Kevin Corcoran was elected as secretary, Peter David as chairman, Dai Jones as team manager with John Davies and Alan Perkins as general committee. Although the club could only continue for senior men, Port Talbot Harriers had been saved.

On a brighter note, John Davies had a 41st birthday to remember when he was able to enter the Welsh Masters Champs for the first time. John won gold in the javelin with 39.20m and silver in the 1500m (4-40.8).

Now the bad news – after a terrific track season in which he set a new division 4 record for the steeplechase and established himself as No.1 Harrier with nine consecutive victories in the club championship, Gareth Edwards left PTH for Cardiff AC.

More bad news – PTH subscriptions were increased from £3 to £5 per annum!

We end 1989 with news of the club championship. Alan Perkins narrowly retained the title he won the previous year and John Davies became the veteran champion.

1990s

The word yo-yo springs to mind when the senior men and the West Glam XC League are mentioned. After being relegated from division 1 the previous season, PTH were immediately promoted back as division 2 champions in March 1990.

Ian Swanson and Geoff Pugh both completed the London Marathon. Ian just had the edge with his 3hrs-09.00 to Geoff's 3hrs-09.30. Mansel Shakeshaft was the M50 winner of the Llanelli Biathlon.

The AGM was held in the Sportsman's Club in March. Kevin Corcoran and Peter David were returned as Secretary and Chairman. John Davies replaced Glan Millard as Treasurer. It was decided to enter a veteran's team in the West Glam XC League with Dai (Ginger) Jones as team manager.

The late summer of 1990 saw an influx of members who took part in the Welsh T&F League. There were some good performances from Vince Lewis, Tim O'Leary, Mike Powell and Andrew David. They came too late, however, to save relegation to division 5.

Secretary, Kevin Corcoran, was busy during the early summer raising sponsorship from PT Council and Kevin Lane (Solicitors) for a 5.75-mile trail race to be held in Pontrhydyfen. The local rugby club also chipped in providing their clubhouse as the base for the race. The event proved successful with many runners from all over South Wales competing and the Mayoress, Cllr Hilda Mears presented the trophies. Paul Richards (Swansea) in 31.05 was the first male winner, and first lady in 39.34 was Frances Gill (Neath). It was very pleasing to hear that port talbot-based Frances was in fine form and was selected to represent Wales at the XC international at Irvine in Scotland on November 3rd.

We end 1990 with the Avlon Motors club championship results. Mike Worlock was the senior men's winner and John Davies retained the veteran's championship.

1991

The West Glam XC Champs were held in January, 1991 at Gnoll Park. Alan Furnell was the only Harrier to gain selection for the county team with a 6th place finish.

Results were mediocre in the top-class Gwent XC League, but PTH managed to hold on to their place in division 1 of the West Glam XC League.

Jeff Rees was disappointed after the London Marathon. Despite setting a new pb of 2hrs30-34, Jeff said he would like to have dipped under the 2-30 mark. On the strength of this run, Jeff, a TA regular, was selected to represent the British Army at the Berlin Marathon later in the year.

At the AGM, the following officers were re-elected: – Kevin Corcoran - Secretary; Peter David - Chairman and John Davies - Treasurer. In view of the increased interest in T&F it was decided to hold a club sprint championship and a best field athlete award in addition to the existing championship. The club was grateful to BP Chemicals, Baglan Bay for donating the trophies for these new awards. Dai (Ginger) Jones) was presented with a tankard for his services to the club. He was off to seek his fortune in Scotland, although there was a strong rumour that there was a lady friend involved!

PTH shook off the disappointment of relegation from division 4 of the Welsh T&F League the previous season to emerge as leaders of division 5 at Carmarthen in May. In top form were Vince Lewis, Richard Lewis, Tim O'Leary and Neill Golding. The 4x100m relay team set a new division 5 record. Later in May, Vince Lewis won the West Glam long jump championship with a leap of 5.36m.

Also in May, Dai Jones realized that there was no place like home and he was warmly welcomed back into the fold!

After being laid up with Achilles tendonitis for five months, John Davies entered the Sandfields Centre Septathlon to test his fitness. John won four of the events and emerged the gold medal winner against much younger opposition.

145 runners took part in the second PTH forestry run at Pontrhydyfen on 31st July, 1991. Justin Hobbs (Cardiff) was the male winner in 28.43 and Liz Francis (36.21), also of Cardiff, was the female winner.

PTH finished 1st in three of the Welsh League matches and 2nd in the fourth to claim the division 5 championship. The sprinters, Vince Lewis, Richard Lewis and Andrew David were in good form throughout the season. Tim O'Leary and Steve Gardner hit the heights over the hurdles. Newcomer, Steve Naunton proved a useful asset in the long jump and triple jump while Jason Roberts set a pb of 4-27.7 in the 1500m. Most of the field events were covered by Tim O'Leary, Andrew Langford, Leigh Francis and Neill Golding. Stalwarts like Alan Perkins, Alan Furnell, John Gill, Carl Mullens and Kevin Corcoran plugged the gaps in the middle-distance races.

Geoff Pugh won gold medals for the M50 800m and triple jump at the Welsh Masters Champs in Morfa, while John Davies recovered from yet another injury just in time to make the Champs and won the M40 Javelin with a throw of 39.78m. John was selected to represent Welsh Masters, along with Alan Perkins, in the Inter-Area match at Reading.

The club was grateful to accept an offer from the Green Stars RFC to use their Little Warren clubhouse as a base for changing and training.

Mike Worlock finished 7th in the West Glam XC Champs at Gnoll Park and was selected to represent the county at Corby in January.

● TEAM manager of the Port Talbot Harriers Athletics Club, Alan Perkins, is presented with the Panasonic Welsh Men's League Division Five trophy by League president, John Collins.

Worthy winner of the new BP Shield Sprint Championship was Neill Golding and Tim O'Leary was the top field eventer. Mike Worlock retained the Men's Champs and Alan Perkins was the Veteran Champion.

1992

Mike Worlock and Kevin Corcoran were the mainstays of the XC leagues in the early part of 1992. PTH maintained their positions in both the West Glam and Gwent Leagues.

The club took on the burden of organizing the West Glam Road Relay Champs on 29th March, based at the Green Stars RFC club. Guest team, Bridgend won, but second placed Neath Harriers were the West Glam Champions.

At the AGM, the following officials were elected: - Secretary – Kevin Corcoran; Chairman – Peter David; Treasurer – John Davies; Team Manager – Alan Perkins; Captain – Neill Golding. Neill was also elected Youth Liaison Officer after qualifying as a field event coach; and thanks to his generosity, a trophy would be awarded to the top points scorer in the Welsh League. The committee were disappointed to announce that top class athlete, Dai Richards was joining Neath Harriers.

PTH just missed out on promotion to division 3 of the Welsh T&F League by finishing 3rd in the final table, although having scored more team points than 2nd placed Aberdare. It was a good team effort with athletes covering multiple events. It was especially pleasing for two athletes in particular. Vince Lewis won the athlete of the day at Colwyn Bay for his sprint double and Steve Naunton for his consistently good long and triple jump efforts. Steve was doubly honoured when he was voted the Field Athlete of the Year for division 4.

Away from the track, Jeff Rees won the Hereford Marathon in June and then won the Roman Run in 1hr50 in September. And back to the track, John Davies won three gold medals at the Welsh Masters Championships in Brecon. The events were: - Javelin (35.28m), 400m H (73.8), Triple jump (8.75m). At the same championships, Ian Swanson came of age and won gold in the M40 long jump (3.86m);

In December, 1992, the presentation night was held at the Green Stars club. Neill Golding retained his Sprint Championship, Steve Naunton was Field Athlete of the Year, Jeff Rees was Senior Men's Champion and Alan Furnell the Veteran Champion.

During 1993, the club kept plodding away in the XC leagues with no movement up or down. Simon Cooper and Alan Perkins were selected for the West Glam team at the Inter-Counties Champs while Kevin Corcoran, Dave Waters, Alan Furnell and Ian Swanson provided the backbone for the league races. There were only two lady members at this stage. Pauline Morris and Alison Roberts who excelled themselves to finish 4th in the final West Glam table out of 10 teams.

Meanwhile, Jeff Rees, in love with long distance running, won the San Domenico 20M (1-51.51) then went on to defend his Hereford Marathon title (2hrs33.33) in June. Dave Waters was the first TRFC club member (47.53) in the Taibach RFC MT8Mile race.

Alison Roberts comfortably won the Aberafan Biathlon held at the Afan Lido in May, 1993. Alison's winning time was 37.40 for the 500m swim and 4 mile run on the seafront.

Veteran Martin Rees won the PTH 5.75M Forestry race outright setting an M40 record of 29.32 in the process. Lisa Carthew, now with Swansea was the lady's winner (35.04).

PTH finished 2nd overall behind Preseli in the Welsh T&F League and gained promotion to division 3. The 'old men' were pleased to finish 2nd to Cardiff in the Welsh Masters League. This was a notable achievement considering the strength of clubs such as Swansea, Neath and Bridgend who all finished below PTH. In the Welsh Masters Champs there was a rich haul of gold medals by Geoff Pugh 800m (2-19.8), 1500m (4-54.9); Jim O'Brien 10k (36-17.2), 5k (17-52.7); Alan Perkins 1500m (4-44.1); Ian Swanson 400mH (84.7), high jump (1.30m) and John Davies javelin (34.22m). John was also presented with the trophy for top points scorer in the Masters League.

Late in 1993, the XC season was hotting up with Simon Cooper and Steve Wilkinson on top form. For the ladies, Pauline Morris and Alison Roberts were improving rapidly. Geoff Pugh was the first M50 runner (29-54) in the Boxing Day Glynneath 5M.

Simon Cooper achieved a remarkable double in winning both the distance and sprint club champs while Alan Perkins retained the Veterans Championship for 1993.

1994

Super running by Simon Cooper and Steve Wilkinson was the key to promotion to division 1 of the Gwent League in March, 1994. There were some solid performances to back them up by Alan Perkins, Kevin Corcoran, Dave Waters and John Ayres which resulted in a table-topping finish to the XC season.

The following officials were elected at the AGM: - Secretary – Kevin Corcoran, Chairman – Peter David, Treasurer – Alan Furnell, Track Team Manager – Alan Perkins, Road Team Manager – Paul Rabaiotti. A development plan was agreed to try and recruit new members, in particular ladies and juniors.

The ever-improving Pauline Morris showed her versatility by winning the Neath Harriers short course triathlon at Llandarcy in May.

PTH lost one of its most dedicated members when Dai Ginger Jones passed away on the 21st May. Athletics was Dai's life and he was always ready to help out coaching, managing or officiating. He was helping at the Melin Fun Run and jogging with a group of youngsters when he collapsed and all efforts to revive him failed. He was ever-present at venues throughout Wales regardless of the weather and his friendly humour made him universally popular.

At the end of May there was further success for Pauline Morris when she was first F35 in the Baglan RFC 5K road race. Newly signed up youngster, Gareth Ayres, won the junior race at Taibach RFC.

The club was very pleased to welcome back Jim O'Brien after spells with Bridgend and Cardiff. Jim lost no time in proving his worth when he was 1st M55 in the Glynneath Opencast 5M. Also in this race Pauline Morris was the 1st F35 and Geoff Pugh 1st M50.

Swansea Harriers made a clean sweep of the PTH 5.75M Forestry Race in August, claiming the top three male and female places in the race. Shaun Tobin won the men's race and Lisa Carthew the lady's race.

Although unable to field a full team in any of the reorganized Welsh T&F League matches, PTH consolidated their place in section A of division 1.

Dai 'Ginger' Jones

Eighteen juniors attended the development day at the Afan Lido. Of these, fourteen turned out in the first Gwent XC race at St Bride's Major in October.

Triathlon seemed to be a fast-developing sport for the Harriers at this time. Mark Howard was the latest to try his hand at this strength-sapping sport. Mark won the Cymmer Afan short course triathlon in a time of 49-28.

Simon Cooper achieved the double of sprint and distance championship titles for a second time and Alan Perkins retained the Veteran's Championship.

1995

Not only did our juniors make their debut in the Gwent XC League, but in January, 1995, three of them ran for West Glam in the Inter-counties Champs at Luton. The speedy three were – Kelly Collins, Rhian Weaver and Gary McCombe.

Tony Holling set a pb of 5hrs12mins in the Barry 40M race. It needed total concentration to run 161 laps of the Jenner Park track and his time was a 23-minute improvement. Tony was rewarded for his efforts with a silver medal for 2nd place.

In March, the officers elected at the AGM were: - President – Jim Mescall, Secretary – Kevin Corocran, Chairman – Peter David, Treasurer – Alan Furnell, T&F Manager – Neill Golding, Road Managers – Paul Rabaiotti and Steve Wilkinson, XC Manager – Alan Perkins, Junior Manager – John Ayres, Junior Press Officer – Gareth Davies, Senior Press Officer – Alan Perkins and Club Champs Organiser – Jeremy Davies.

Pauline Morris was a comfortable winner in the Multisport Racing Club's 10K (40.34) at Neath in June.

During the summer of 1995, the juniors were starting to make their presence felt. Gareth Ayres won the javelin in an open meeting, Kelly and Justin Collins were boy's and girl's winners in the 2M races at the Valley Festival.

The senior men consolidated their place in the Welsh T&F League while the old men finished 2nd behind Swansea in the Masters League.

In their first attempt at the Welsh Castles Relay, PTH finished a creditable 18th. Steve Wilkinson was the star, finishing 5th on the final leg from Caerphilly Castle to Cardiff Castle.

Winners of the PTH Forestry Run at Pontrhydyfen were Martin Rees (Swansea) and Francis Gill (Newport). Pauline Morris was pleased as punch to win the F35 race.

Bad news for the club at the end of 1995 – Kevin Corcoran had moved to Swansea to live and resigned as secretary; Steve Wilkinson transferred to Bridgend. Alan Perkins was elected to replace Kevin Corcoran as secretary.

There were double celebrations for two of our top athletes at the end-of-year presentation evening. Simon Cooper was Open club and Sprint champion; Tony Holling won the Veteran Open and Veteran Sprint championships.

1996

The only highlight of the 1996 XC Leagues for the men was Steve Wilkinson's win at Morfa, running second claim for PTH. However, Pauline Morris was in scintillating form for the ladies team winning 4 out of 5 of the West Glam races and taking the individual title as well. Tony Holling was very happy with his 3hrs10 time in the London Marathon. Mark Davies was even happier to record 2hrs51 – a pb by 27 minutes.

Promising youngster, Geraint Davies won the junior Briton Ferry race, then ran in the Ferry 5M race an hour later. Geraint won his second trophy of the day when he was 1st U21 runner home.

At the AGM Alan Perkins was elected as Secretary, Peter David – Chairman, John Ayres – Treasurer and Jim Mescall - President

There was no movement in the Welsh T&F League. The ancient members overcame their stiff joints to finish second below Swansea again in the Welsh Masters League. Despite winning all the javelin events, John Davies could only finish second to Brian Barratt (Neath) in the top points scoring table.

Winners of the PTH 5.75M Forestry Race were Martin Rees (Swansea) and Francis Gill (Newport). Gareth Robbins (Swansea, son of Dil) and Tracy Andrews (Neath) won the junior races.

John Ayres showed a tidy turn of speed to win three of the five races and take the club Sprint Championship and Tony Holling took the Veteran Sprint title. Paul Rabaiotti won the Senior Men's Championship and Alan Perkins the Veteran's title.

Tony Holling, Welsh Team Captain, Celtic Plate 100K, Edinburgh, 1997

In 1997, Tony Holling, Dave Waters and Alan Perkins were in pretty good form in the XC leagues. An unusual situation occurred in the WGXC League when the senior men's team was relegated to division 2 and the veteran's team was promoted to division 1. Also in excellent form was Pauline Morris who was the overall winner of the F35 individual championship in the Gwent League.

Class will out and as an ultra-runner, Tony Holling proved his class by winning the Barry 40M race in March. Tony's excellent time of 4hrs 48-23, a pb by 23 minutes, earned him selection as captain for the Welsh Ultra Team. Tony was also 1st M40 in the open section of the race.

Dean Hannaford, who joined PTH in 1996 and made rapid progress, was selected for Welsh Colleges and finished a very creditable 8th in a top-class field at the Colleges XC Championships.

At the AGM, officers elected were: - Secretary – Alan Perkins, Chairman – Peter David, Treasurer – John Ayres.

The summer T&F leagues were poorly attended for various reasons and results were mediocre to say the least. The 3K steeplechase is a gruelling event and not a very popular one. However, to gain points for their club quite a few athletes would try it – at least once. A league meeting in Barry was made quite memorable when a youngster from Beddau, who shall remain nameless, decided to try his luck. He gamely hurdled the barriers when most runners would step on and off them. The water jump was always a step onto the barrier and push off hard to avoid a soaking. After a couple of laps this boy, in his enthusiasm, hurdled the barrier at the water jump. To his amazement – and the spectator's amusement – he fell up to his neck in the muddy depths of the waters below! To his credit he emerged dripping wet and finished the race.

John Ayres retained his Sprint Championship. The in-form Tony Holling won the open Championship and Alan Perkins was unstoppable, taking the Veteran's title once more.

1998

In 1998, PTH maintained their places in both XC leagues. Tony Holling and Dean Hannaford represented Wales. Both had to retire from these races, Tony with stomach pains and Dean with respiratory problems. Both athletes made a rapid recovery and were soon back running again. Tony had an appendectomy! Tony also went on to run for Wales in the Celtic Plate 100K International in France and helped the Welsh team to 2nd place.

At the AGM, the following officers were elected: - Secretary – Alan Perkins, Chairman – Peter David, Treasurer/Membership Sec – John Davies.

With all the members doing multiple events, PTH finished 2nd in the Welsh T&F League, winning promotion to division 3. The oldsters finished 4th in the Masters League with John Davies as the league's top points scorer. John also won gold medals in the Masters Championships for Javelin (36.39m), 800m (2-33.5) and 1500m (5-11.5) and was also 1st M50 in the Cymerafan Short Course Triathlon.

Simon Cooper again achieved the double of Sprint and Open Club Championships while Alan Perkins retained his Veteran's title.

1999

Simon Cooper was still top of the pops in 1999. He took an early lead in the club championship and finished in the top ten of every WGXC League race. His consistency won him the overall individual championship in the West Glam as well. PTH were placed 3rd in division 3 of the Gwent XC League.

There was a good turnout for the WGXC Championships and it was pleasing to see new member, Emily Crowley, finishing in 5th place to gain selection for the county team. Emily won individual silver and team gold at the Inter-Counties and went on to also run for Wales. Also selected for the county were Simon Cooper, Gareth Ayres and Ross Bamsey. Gareth and Ross helped the U17 team to win the gold medal at the Inter-Counties.

Tony Holling was also in fine form. He finished 3rd in the Barry 40M and again represented Wales in the 100K Celtic Plate Trophy International in Dublin.

At the AGM the officers elected were: - Secretary – Alan Perkins, Chairman – Peter David and Treasurer/Membership Sec – John Davies.

Welsh Athletics decided to combine the women's and men's T&F leagues in 1999. This made no difference to PTH who remained in division 4. The veterans finished 4th in the Masters League and John Davies won 3 gold medals in the M50 Championships for 100m (14.7), 200m (29.4) and javelin (34.63m).

Youngster, Ross Bamsey, showed Simon Cooper a clean pair of heels in three of the club sprint races to claim the title of Club Sprint Champion. There was no holding Simon over the longer distances though and he won the open championship by a long margin. Alan Perkins claimed the veteran's title once more.

2000s

Simon Cooper was once again top dog during the XC season ending in March 2000. The senior men's team finished 5th in division 1 of the WGXC League but the veteran's team propped up the table and were relegated to division 2. There was, however, good news in the Gwent League. PTH finished 2nd in division 3 and were promoted to division 2; Mel James was the M50 top points scorer. There was bad news as well – Emily Crowley, after winning the U17 Gwent race at Margam Park, left PTH for Swansea.

There was something to shout about for PTH in the Richard Burton 10K. Jim O'Brien was 1st M50 (although by now he was over 60!) and Gareth Ayres and Ross Bamsey took the top two places in the junior 4K race.

Despite having no ladies competing in the combined Men/Women's T&F League, PTH managed to win Division 3 through the efforts of the athletes being prepared to turn out in multiple events. All the clubs did this to cover as many events as possible. The veterans took 3rd place in their league. The team of Mel James, Jim O'Brien, Ian Swanson and John Davies set a new Welsh Masters record of 59.7 for the M50 4x100m relay at Neath in May. Ian Swanson won M50 gold for the high jump (1.25m) at the Welsh Masters Champs and John Davies won gold medals for javelin (35.84m) and discus (23.72m) and represented Welsh Masters at the Inter-Area match in Grantham, Lincolnshire.

A curious incident occurred in the 3000m race at the second Master's League. All the athletes ran an extra lap by mistake. The times were invalid, but Jeff Rees, who won the race was advised that he should claim a new Welsh record for the 3400m race!

Jim O'Brien won the M60 category at the Cardiff 10K and was selected for the Welsh Masters team for the XC International in Ireland later in the year.

Twinkle-toed Ross Bamsey was in sparkling form in the club Sprint Champs, winning all five races to retain his title. Simon Cooper won the open Championship and Alan Perkins the Veteran's title.

And on a festive note, PTH won the Father Christmas Team Trophy at the Glynneath 5M on Boxing Day thanks to the efforts of John Hopkins, Tony Holling and Alan Perkins!

2001

There was an outbreak of Foot & Mouth disease at the start of 2001 which curtailed the XC season. The WGXC scheduled for Gnoll Park was transferred to Aberafan Beach instead. Mel James was M50 top points scorer in the West Glam for the second time.

PTH remained static in the Welsh T&F League and the pensioners were runners-up to Cardiff in the Masters T&F League. Highlights of the T&F season were a gold medal for Ian Swanson for the high jump (1.25M) in the West Glam Champs and he also went on to win gold medals at the Welsh Masters Champ with a 1.25m high jump and 7.26m triple jump There was also a gold for John Davies in the javelin (35.94m). John went on to represent Welsh Masters in the Inter-Area Match at Moorway Stadium, Derby. He was also delighted to receive the Matt Cullen Trophy for Best Thrower in the Welsh Masters League.

There was sad news in June when it was announced that club president, Jim Mescall, had passed away at the relatively early age of 72. Jim had been a staunch supporter of the Harriers and regularly attended the presentation evenings.

Simon Cooper took advantage of Ross Bamsey's absence to win all five of the club Sprint Championship races. Simon again achieved the double by winning the Open Champs as well. Alan Perkins took the Veteran's title once more.

There was a warm welcome in November for David Oak and Colin Anthony who both transferred from Neath to PTH.

In December 2001, the committee decided to ask Glan Francis to be the club's new president and were delighted to acknowledge his acceptance. Glan had been a PTH coach and was the father of club members Helen and Leigh Francis.

A postscript for 2001 – Alan Perkins was 1st M50 at the Glynneath 5M and Tony Holling won 1st prize for fancy dress!

2002

The XC season ended in March 2002 with the senior men being relegated to join the veterans in division 2 of the West Glam XC League. The one bright spot was that Alan Perkins was M50 top points scorer.

At the AGM the officers elected were: - President – Glan Francis, Secretary – Alan Perkins, Chairman – Peter David, Treasurer/Memb Sec – John Davies.

PTH Winners of Welsh Masters T&F League, 2002

The Veteran's T&F team had an influx of new members which meant that most events were covered throughout the season. The new members included Mike Davies, Gerry Hunt, Alan Mann and Richard Boon, all second claim from Les Croupiers who didn't have a

T&F team. Consistent winners were Alan Perkins in the 1500m and John Davies in the javelin. John went on to win gold in the Masters Champs and both he and Alan Perkins represented Welsh Masters at the Inter-Area match in Tidworth where John produced a throw of 43.36m to win the gold medal. PTH went on to win the Welsh Masters League with a massive total of 903 points.

Highlight of the autumn was the win by Louise Copp in the WGXC race at Margam Park. Louise was running as second claim for PTH.

Alan Perkins took full advantage of the absence of the injured Ross Bamsey and Simon Cooper to claim both the club Sprint and Open Champs. Tony Holling was the winner of the Veteran's title.

2003

In the continued absence of Simon Cooper in 2003, Carl Ellis and Steve Rees were the front runners on the XC scene. The senior men were promoted to division 1 of the West Glam, but were relegated to division 3 of the Gwent League after finishing bottom of division 2.

Tony Holling was 5th in the Barry 40M and represented Wales again in the Celtic Plate 100K.

At the AGM officers elected were: - President - Glan Francis, Secretary – Alan Perkins, Chairman – Peter David, Treasurer/Memb Sec – John Davies, Kit Secretary – John Davies.

In a mediocre track season, the seniors finished 3rd in division 3 of the Welsh League and the veterans also finished 3rd in the Masters League. Ian Swanson was making a habit of winning gold for the high jump in the Welsh Masters Champs and this year was no exception when he won with a leap of 1.20m. John Davies won two gold medals for M50 javelin (38.60m) and discus (23.72m). John represented Welsh Masters at the Inter-Area Match in Victoria Park, Warrington where he won the M50 javelin gold medal with a throw of 38.78m.

Ross Bamsey was back to his best after injury and won all five races to take the club Sprint Championship once more. Alan Perkins was Open Champion and Tony Holling claimed the veteran title.

2004

There was quite an influx of new members towards the end of 2003 and beginning of 2004. Charles Walsh, Len Richards, Ray James, Mark Morris, Mark Taylor, Tim and Amanda Elias all joined the club.

In the West Glam XC League the senior men were promoted to division 1, but the veterans were relegated to division 2. PTH finished 4th in division 3 of the Gwent League. Ian Swanson achieved the remarkable record of 100 consecutive Gwent XC races. That meant not missing a single race for 20 years!

Tony Holling took on a new coaching role for the 2004 Barry 40M and helped Amanda Elias to win the ladies' race.

There wasn't much interest in the Welsh T&F League where PTH languished near the bottom of division 3. Les Croupiers entered a team in the Masters League so all their members were unable to compete for PTH leaving the club floundering in 4th place. John Davies won three gold medals at the Masters Champs for javelin (38.04m), 800m (2-49.5) and 1500m (5-59.0), and went on to represent Welsh Masters at the Inter-Area match in Stockwood Park, Luton where he collected the javelin silver medal.

The XC season came around once more in the autumn of 2004 and there was a good turnout for the West Wales Champs. Steve Rees, Carl Ellis, Gareth Ayres, Dave Williams and Len Richards all earned selection for the area team.

The rapidly improving Charles Walsh won all five races to take the club Sprint Championship and showed his versatility by winning the Open Champs as well. Len Richards won the Veteran Champs.

Talking about veterans, the team of Kevin Corcoran, Alan Perkins, John Hopkins and Ray James won the Veteran Team Trophy at the Glynneath 5M on Boxing Day. This was no mean achievement considering two of the team were in fancy dress!

2005

In 2005, there were mixed fortunes in the West Glam League. Bad news - the senior men were relegated to division 2; good news - after topping division 2 the veterans were promoted to division 1.

At the AGM officers elected were: - President – Glan Francis, Secretary – Alan Perkins, Chairman – Peter David, Treasurer/Kit Sec/membership – John Davies.

The T&F season ended with PTH firmly entrenched in division 3 of the Welsh League while the veterans managed 3rd place in the Masters League. John Davies collected four gold medals in the Welsh Masters Champs in Cardiff – javelin (35.88m), discus (25.06m), hammer (24.78m) and shot (7.35m). He was selected to represent Welsh Masters in Solihull, but was away on holiday and could not compete. In November a special award was made to Alan Perkins and John Davies. They were presented with inscribed Indian clubs as Welsh Masters Clubmen of the Year for their commitment to PTH in T&F and XC.

Charles Walsh, Steve Rees and Carl Ellis were the front runners in the Open Club Champs with Charles coming out on top and also winning all five of the races to take the Sprint Champs again. Len Richards won the veteran title.

2006

In 2006, Steve Rees, Charles Walsh, Carl Ellis, Steve Wilkinson and Gareth Ayres were all in good form. Because of unavailability, this was not reflected in the XC leagues where PTH made no movement.

Steve Rees had made the most rapid improvement. He won the Sarn Helen 10M race in a swift 55-30 and went on to run the Cardiff marathon in a superb pb of 2hrs-38.21.

Tony Holling was back in long distance mode and ran the Barry 40M in 5hrs-36.05. He was 2nd senior and 1st M50 resulting in his selection for the Welsh team at the 100k Celtic Plate International.

At the AGM officers elected were: - President – Glan Francis, Secretary/membership – Alan Perkins, Chairman – Peter David, Treasurer/Kit – John Davies.

There was little interest in the T&F leagues in 2006. The senior men's team languished in division 3 of the Welsh League and the veterans finished 4th in the Masters League. John Davies won gold medals in the Welsh Masters Champs for javelin (34.99m), discus (26.15m), and hammer (24.18m).

It was sad to record the passing of Port Talbot-born Roy Bish in November, 2006. Roy had been a member of PTYM during the 1950s and had gone on to play rugby for Aberafan and become a noted athletics and rugby coach. He was the first qualified coach in charge of Cardiff RFC from 1965 to 1980. Quality players like Maurice Richards, Keri Jones, Gerald Davies, Gareth Edwards and Barry John had prospered under his guidance.

Gareth Ayres showed a tidy turn of speed to win two of the club sprint races. Charles Walsh was 2nd in both those, but went on to win the remaining three races and took the Club Sprint Champs again and also made it a double by winning the Open title. Len Richards was the Club Veteran Champion once more. A new innovation in 2006 was the introduction of a Lady's Club Sprint Championship which was deservedly won by Jenny Grey.

2007

The XC season 2006/7 was a successful one for the senior men. They topped the WGXC League division 2 table and were promoted to division 1. Carl Ellis was in great form and was the Individual Overall Winner. Carol Mosely and Judith Oakley had recently joined PTH and were promising to be very able runners. Gareth Ayres, Charles Walsh and Chris Fulcher all ran for West Wales at the Inter-Counties Champs in Nottingham.

The T&F side of the club was still in the doldrums with only Alan Perkins, Ian Swanson and John Davies making regular appearances in the Welsh League and Mel James and Tony Holling joining them for the Masters Leagues. They were also joined by 73-year-old Len Tew who had renewed his membership after a long absence. Len had been part of the Welsh Marathon winning team back in 1963. John Davies went on to win the M55 javelin gold medal at the Welsh Masters Champs and was selected for the Inter-Area match, but couldn't attend because of injury. Later in the year he was awarded the Dave Williams Commemorative Trophy for his outstanding contribution to Welsh Masters Athletics.

Steve Rees was in exceptional form during 2007, winning the Ammanford 10K (34-54) and the Coytrahen 3K (9-36). Steve, Charles Walsh and Carl Ellis won the team trophy at Ammanford and Carol Moseley was 2nd lady (46-51).

Tony Holling couldn't stay away from the Barry 40M. He was 2nd overall (5hrs36-05) and 1st M50. As a result, he was selected for Wales once more in the Celtic Plate 100K International. Later in the year he achieved his ambition of running the 90K Comrades Marathon in South Africa.

In September, 2007 a party of senior and very senior men took a trip up north for the Anglesey Marathon. It was a tough course, with the last couple of miles being almost all uphill. It held no fear for Alan Perkins though who sailed through in 3hrs 42-12 to win the M55 Welsh Masters title.

Charles Walsh won four out of five of the races to claim the club Sprint Championship and also won the Open Champs as well. Keiran McIntosh won the other sprint race. Alan Perkins regained the Veteran title and Carol Mosely won the Lady's Sprint Champs.

2008

The highlight of the XC season was the impact made by our ladies. Carol Moseley was 3rd in the final West Glam fixture and Judith Oakley was the overall F40 individual winner. It was also remarkable that with just these two competing, PTH finished 4th team in the league!

The senior men had seen a boost in their numbers. Excellent packing in the Llanelli Half Marathon gave PTH the team gold medal. Leading the team home in 19th place was Adrian Weaver (1-22.57), 22nd Chris Fulcher (1-23.30) and 24th Nigel Barnes (1-23.47). Another new member, who has developed into one of the club's best coaches, was Paul Jelley.

On a Tuesday evening in April, Bernie Henderson was doing his final training run before competing in the London Marathon the following Sunday. Bernie wasn't aware at the time that he was running around the PTH speedwork area until he was approached by Alan Perkins. In his own inimitable way, Alan asked if Bernie would like to join PTH. Bernie was 53 and thought it was too late in life for him to join an athletics club. Alan replied that he was 57 and his friendly attitude won Bernie over. What a lucky and momentous meeting that was for PTH!

At the AGM the following officers were re-elected: - President - Glan Francis, Secretary/Membership – Alan Perkins, Chairman – Peter David, Treasurer/Kit – John Davies.

PTH were just holding their own in the Welsh League during the summer of 2008. The veterans finished 3rd in the Masters League. Vince Lewis, who was an accomplished and speedy soccer player and had been a member in his earlier days, returned to the fold with great effect. At the Welsh Masters Champs Vince won the 400m gold (55.6) and was selected for Welsh Masters at the Inter-Area match in Hemel Hempstead. Alan Perkins was also selected while, despite a niggling injury, John Davies won three gold medals for javelin (25.90m), discus (25.54m), hammer (25.37m) and was also selected for Welsh Masters. The injury, however, prevented his attendance.

In September a party of Harriers made the trip north again for the Anglesey Marathon and stayed overnight in the aptly named Ty Hapus guesthouse. The landlord was a Jim Royle (The Royle Family) look-alike and had everyone in stitches. Mother and daughter duo of Elvira and Carol Moseley joined the trip, so the boys were on their best behaviour! Carol was running her first marathon and was paced by Alan Perkins to a respectable 3hrs51 time which also gave Alan the M55 Welsh Marathon gold medal again.

Steve Rees was unable to compete on a regular basis because he was a North Sea worker. He made up for his absence when he came home by winning the Coytrahen 3k (9-27) and the Sarn Helen Race (1hr-48.56).

No one could match Vince Lewis's blistering pace and he won all five races to take the Club Sprint Championship. Carol Moseley was the Lady's Sprint Champion. Carl Ellis won the Open Club Champs and Chris Fulcher gained the reward of his tough training regime to take the Veteran title.

2009

At the end of 2008 and beginning of 2009 the lady's membership increased significantly. Tina Arthur, Yvonne Brown, Mandy Morris, Clare Phillips, Sandra Pinkham, Ceri Brambley-Tucker and Pauline Williams all joined PTH. With runners of such calibre joining Carol Mosely and Judith Oakley the result was inevitable – the lady's team easily won division 1 of the West Glam XC League.

Ian Swanson was nothing if not consistent in his attendance at the Gwent XC League. He achieved the remarkable record of 125 consecutive races – 25 years without missing a race. John Davies couldn't catch up with him, but had just achieved 75 consecutive races.

At the AGM there was little change: - President – Glan Francis, Secretary – Alan Perkins, Chairman – Peter David, Treasurer/Kit/Membership – John Davies.

Steve Rees made the most of his visit home in June. In a swift 33-37 he won the Llanelli 10K race.

The senior men's team languished near the bottom of division 3 in the Welsh League while the veterans managed 3rd in the Masters League. Having just turned 60, John Davies brought home a bonanza of gold medals in the Welsh Masters Champs – javelin (38.44m), discus (28.98m), Hammer (26.21m), shot (7.44m), 800m (2-59.4) and 1500m (6-01.7). Alan Perkins and John Davies were selected for the Welsh Masters team at the Inter-Area Match in Solihull, but John preferred to attend his son's wedding.

PTH Winners West Glam XC League, 2008/9

There was sad news in October. Johnny O'Brien, third born son of Ike, passed away at the comparatively early age of 70. Johnny was an extremely able runner in his early days and continued to compete in local races well into his 40s. (I had many a battle with Johnny. He was always good-natured and encouraging whether I beat him or he beat me.)

The Open Club Championship was won by the consistent and competitive Charles Walsh while Chris Fulcher took the Veteran's title again.

By this time the local newspapers had ceased production. Communication was largely through the internet and information was hard to find – so here ends the tale of 2009.

2010s

Well done our brilliant ladies team – top of division 1 West Glam XC League and top of division 3 in the Gwent League which meant promotion to division 2. The men's teams consolidated their positions in both the West Glam and Gwent Leagues.

David Oak had a happy start to the new year when he collected a silver medal for his efforts at the Old Father Time Welsh 5M championship in Cardiff.

Len Tew had just turned 75 which seemed to revitalize him! At the British Masters Indoor Champs in March, he won the 800m (2-56.45) and 1500m (6-00.10). At the British Masters Outdoor Champs in July, he won the 400m (74.20), 800m (3-26.18) and 1500m (6-07.68). At the Welsh Masters Champs in August, he had an easy day only competing in the 800m, but winning that race as well! Also at the Welsh Masters Champs there were gold medals for Vince Lewis – M40 400m; Ian Swanson – M60 high jump, triple jump and long jump; John Davies – M60 javelin (35.88m), hammer (25.68m), discus (31.14m) and shot (7.75m). John was also selected for Welsh Masters at the Inter-Area Match in Solihull.

In June PTH entered a mixed team in the Welsh Castles Relay for the first time since 1995, finishing 28th (25hrs19mins). Highlight of the trip was the club's own house-band with entertainment provided by Alan Roberts, Ray James and John Ayres!

We welcomed former Swansea athlete Clare Phillips to PTH during 2010. Clare was in fine form, winning amongst other races the Welsh 5K Champs in Swansea (18-57), Brecon 10-

mile (65-49) and the Dale Half Marathon (1hr26-23). Ian Swanson also won M60 gold at the 5K (28.00) in Swansea.

With the return of cross country in the autumn of 2010, the ladies were still in fine form topping the West Glam table. Sandra Pinkham was our leading runner and was selected for Welsh Masters at the XC International in Dublin.

Apologies for not having found any information about our club sprint champs. Winners of the open champs: - Women – Sandra Pinkham, Vet Women – Ceri Brambley-Tucker; Men – Gareth Ayres, Vet Men – Chris Fulcher.

Len Tew, 2010 M75 British Champion 400m, 800m, 1500m

With Sandra Pinkham to the fore again our ladies completed a hat trick of wins in the West Glam XC League in March 2011. Sandra was 1st lady at Llanmadoc and Gnoll Park and also the Individual Overall Winner at the end of the season. The ladies consolidated their place in division 2 of the Gwent League, placing 4th, and Sandra was 3rd F45 in the individual table. Not to be outdone, the men's team also won division 1 of the West Glam League. There was an influx of new members in 2010/11 which included Chris Parker who won the M45 Individual Overall Trophy.

2011

The presentation night was held on 12th February to coincide with the 50th anniversary of Port Talbot Harriers which developed out of the PTYMCA Harriers in 1961. Guests of Honour were Dillwyn Robbins, Jim O'Brien and Len Tew who, in 1963, had won the team event at the Welsh Marathon Champs.

The lack of interest in the T&F leagues continued with only the usual suspects competing. Ian Swanson won gold for the M60 high jump (1.10m) at the Welsh Masters Champs while John Davies collected four golds at M60 for javelin (32.00m), hammer (26.07m), discus (28.36m) and shot (6.75m). Alan Perkins, Pauline Williams and John Davies were all selected for the Welsh Masters team at the Inter-Area Match in Solihull.

Clare Phillips had rapidly established herself as top of the pops at PTH. During 2011 she put together a series of superb runs on the road and multi terrain. Clare recorded wins at the Llanelli Marathon (2hr 53-31), Dale Half Marathon (1hr 25-18), (Brecon 10-mile (64-02), Whitford Point (25-05), Aberdare 10K (37-52) and the Roman Run (1hr 56-00).

At the AGM in July, Alan Perkins stood down as secretary and was replaced by Mario Rabaiotti. The other officers were: - Chairman Peter David, Treasurer/kit/membership – John Davies, 1st team XC Captain – Chris Fulcher, 2nd team – Tony Holling, Lady's Team – Pauline Williams. It was also decided to enter a team for the Welsh Castles Relay again with Colin Anthony as Team Manager.

In August Steve Rees set a new club championship record of 1hr-13.49 when he stormed away from the rest of the field in our half marathon.

When the XC season came around again in the autumn, both lady's and men's teams got off to a flying start in the West Glam League. Chris Fulcher was in outstanding form winning the M 40 silver medal at the Welsh Masters XC Champs and earning selection for the Welsh Masters team at the International in Glasgow. The team of Colin Anthony, Alan Perkins and John Davies also won M60 silver medals at the Welsh Masters XC Champs.

In a 5-mile handicap event, organized by Colin Anthony from the Green Stars Club, John Ayres won an exciting and keenly contested race.

Club XC Champions were: - Senior Women – Pauline Williams, Vet Women – Sandra Pinkham, Senior Men – Chris Fulcher, Vet Men – Alan Perkins. Open Club Championship winners were: - Women – Sandra Pinkham, Vet women – Ceri Brambley-Tucker, Men – Gareth Ayres, Vet Men - Paul Rees. Sprint Championship: - Women – Charlotte Hunt, Vet Women – Mandy Morris; Men – Charles Walsh, Vet Men – Alan Roberts.

2012

In 2012 it was another victory for our lady's team in the West Glam XC League, topping division 1 for the 4th consecutive year. Sandra Pinkham won the first race at Llanmadoc and Clare Phillips won three of the remaining four at Margam Park, Tata Steel and Gnoll Park. Sandra was also the Overall Individual winner for the second time. It was a super season for PTH, the men taking the top prize in division 1 of their league as well. There was no movement in the Gwent League, but Alan Perkins was 3rd M60 in the individual overall list. A new venture for PTH was hosting the West Glam XC race at Margam Park with John Davies as race director.

In March 2012 Steve Rees recorded a superb pb of 1hr11-50 when finishing 3rd overall in the Llanelli Half Marathon. Steve was not satisfied with this and claimed another pb of 1hr10-56 in the Cardiff Half Marathon later in the year. Gareth Ayres was also on form in this race recording 1hr14-45 for another pb.

Clare Phillips continued in great form on the roads winning the John Hartson (Llanelli) 10k (38-22), Swansea 5K (18-50), Ammanford 10K (39-42), Brecon 10-mile (63-54) and the Sospan MT10 (67-36). In the Snowdon Marathon Clare was second overall and 1st F35 (3hrs 07-50).

The T&F leagues seemed to hold little interest for the majority of the members. The three aging musketeers Alan Perkins, Ian Swanson and John Davies still continued to compete though. John Davies could only manage one gold medal at the Welsh Masters Champs in his usual javelin event (30.96m). Alan and John were both selected for Welsh Masters at the Inter- Area Match in Solihull.

At the AGM Peter David stood down after doing sterling service as chairman for 23 years. Bernie Henderson took over as chairman. Other officers were: - Secretary – Mario Rabaiotti, Treasurer/kit/membership – John Davies, Lady's Captain – Pauline Williams, Men's Captain – Chris Fulcher, Gwent League shared captaincy – Chris Fulcher and Gareth Ayres, Men's second team renamed The Wizards, captained by Tony Holling, Gwent Team Manager – John Davies.

In June 2012, team manager, Colin Anthony, took his 20-strong team to compete in the Welsh Castles Relay. There was some determined running from the individual members which gave PTH 24th place in a very strong field of 59 clubs. The highlight was Steve Rees' remarkable performance in winning the 12.8mile 15th leg in a time of 68-17. Gareth Ayres was also in excellent form finishing 2nd overall, but 1st male runner on the 9.1mile 18th leg behind international athlete Louise Damen (Winchester). Both Steve and Gareth were awarded yellow t-shirts as leg winners.

The rapidly improving Gareth Ayres was running into a vein of good form. At the Tenby 10K in July, he was neck and neck with Celtic Tri athlete, James Hockin, until the final hill. Gareth put in a strong surge to win by just a few seconds in 34-48.

At the Ammanford 10K, the team of Nigel Barnes (7th, 37-08), Alex Williams (8th, 37-37) and Paul Rees 14th, 39-15) took the team gold medal.

Clare Phillips won the West Glam race at Llanmadoc in November and the ladies continued their dominance of division 1.

Winners of the club champs were: -
Sprints Women – Judith Oakley, Vet Women – Mandy Morris, Men – Neil Marvin, Vet Men – Alex Williams.

XC Women – Mandy Morris, Vet Women – Pauline Williams, Men – Alan Perkins, Vet Men –
Dave Cornish.

Open Women – Sandra Pinkham, Vet Women – Mandy Morris, Men – Gareth Ayres, Vet Men
– Mario Rabaiotti.

     2012 ended with Colin Anthony's 5-mile Handicap Race. The overall winner was guest
Anthony O'Callaghan. With no known form, Anthony was given a generous handicap and
took full advantage of it! First PTH member was Tony Holling.

Clare Phillips Welsh Masters XC International 2013/14/15

2013

Claire Phillips started 2013 with a bang winning the Prince of Wales race on New Year's Day.
She then went on to win the West Glam XC race at Tata Steel 12 days later. The ladies were
unbeatable as a team and recorded their 5th consecutive West Glam title. There was no

movement for the men's team in either the West Glam or the Gwent League. PTH again hosted the West Glam League at Margam Park with John Davies as race director.

There was bad news for PTH though when Chris Fulcher and Steve Rees decided to leave the club and seek their fortunes with Neath Harriers.

T&F was almost non-existent at this time except for the three wise old men! Even they didn't attend the Welsh League, all of them being over 60 now and not wanting to show up the young men in this league! At the Welsh Masters Champs, Ian Swanson won the high jump (1.05m) and John Davies won javelin (29.45m), discus (22.84m), hammer (22.94m), 1500m (7-00.17). Alan Perkins and John Davies were both selected for Welsh Masters at the Inter-Area Match in Solihull.

There was sad news at the beginning of July when club president, Glan Francis, passed away at the age of 81. His connection with PTH went way back to when his son, Leigh, and daughter, Helen, were both members of the club. He regularly attended meetings until his health failed and his passing was a sad loss to PTH.

At the AGM officers elected were: - Chairman – Bernie Henderson, Secretary – Mario Rabaiotti, Treasurer/kit/membership – John Davies; general committee – John Ayres, Carol Moseley, Karl Eenmaa, Tony Holling, Paul Jelley, Amanda Parry, Mandy Morris, Paul Robbins and Alan Roberts. Team Captains, men – Gareth Ayres, 2nd team – John Ayres, Ladies – Pauline Williams. Colin Anthony organized another successful trip to the Welsh Castles Relay, but decided to stand down on returning home. The following WCR sub-committee was elected – Paul Rees, David Parfitt, Karl Eenmaa, Steve Dinham, Ian Williams, Carol Moseley and Amanda Parry. It was decided to approach Port Talbot Town Cricket Club regarding some form of partnership. Paul Rees volunteered to investigate coaching courses.

The 'Have Fun and Run' project initiated by Bernie Henderson earlier in the year proved very successful. It led to a significant increase in the numbers aided by the dedication of the newly qualified coaches under the guidance of Paul Rees.

The sprints championship was cancelled due mainly to the very poor condition of the Western Avenue track and also a lack of T&F sprinters in the club.

Ian Swanson achieved the fantastic record of 150 consecutive Gwent XC races. That's 30 years without missing a single race!

In the autumn an agreement was reached with the cricket club allowing PTH to use a portacabin alongside their clubhouse. At the first committee meeting there it was proposed that former chairman, Peter David, should be offered the position of President. Peter was delighted to accept.

Gareth Ayres was in fine form winning the 15-mile Bwystfil y Bryn race (1hr-31.39) by over three minutes from the second runner. He was also the winner of the 16.5mile Sarn Helen race in a time of 1hr50-33.

No race winners, but our ladies continued to out-perform all the other teams in the West Glam XC League. Clare Phillips won the Ammanford 10k again (41-02) and was 2nd in the Glynneath 5-mile (32-15). Clare was also selected for Welsh Masters at the British XC International in Cardiff.

In October 2013, Tony Holling organized the Hilly Reverse 4 from the Bryn Bettws Bike Centre in Tonmawr.

Another departure – Carol Moseley left Wales in September to take up a teaching and translating post near Madrid in Spain.

Club Championship winners were: -

XC Women – Mandy Morris, Vet Women – Pauline Williams

XC Men – Alan Perkins, Vet Men – John Davies.

Sprints Women – Judith Oakley, Vet Women – Colleen O'Leary

Sprints Men – Luke Price, Vet Men – Alex Williams.

Open Women – Judith Oakley, Vet Women – Mandy Morris

Open Men – Gareth Ayres, Vet Men – Alan Perkins.

Gareth Ayres, Captain & consistent winner of Club Championships

<u>*2014*</u>

Our super ladies team claimed their 6th consecutive West Glam XC title in March 2014 and Mandy Morris was the F40 Individual Overall Winner. There were no race winners, it was all down to consistent turnouts and good team packing. This could not be said for the Gwent League though. They failed to field a team and didn't feature there. The men's team remained static in both leagues.

No Welsh T&F League, but the three amigos still competed fiercely in the Masters League! At the Welsh Masters Champs there was a gold medal for Ian Swanson in the high jump (1.15m) and two gold medals for John Davies in the javelin (28.72m), 1500m (6-33.7) plus a silver in the age-graded pentathlon. Charles Walsh made a rare appearance in the Masters Champs to excellent effect. He won gold medals for 100m (13.1), 800m (2-19.30) and 1500m (4-59.1). Alan P and John D were both selected for Welsh Masters at the Inter - Area Match in Solihull.

In April, 2014, Gareth Ayres ran a superb 2hrs-45.14 pb in the London Marathon. In July he was a comfortable winner of the Ammanford 10K (35.38) and went on to win our PTH half marathon (1hr-20.08) in August.

In June, Alex Williams enjoyed his trip to the Welsh Castles Relay and was surprised to learn that he'd won the yellow t-shirt as 1st M45. Alex ran the 7.7M 19th leg in 48.39 for 9th place overall in a field of 64 starters.

Early in July, Bernie Henderson reluctantly announced that he was going to stand down as chairman at the next AGM. He was finding it increasingly difficult to commit as much time to the club, given its rapid growth over the last two years. Judith Oakley was the only person to volunteer for the post. By popular demand, Bernie was persuaded to change his mind, so there were two candidates for chairperson. At the AGM Judith was elected on the strength of a number of email votes. Other officers elected were: - Secretary – Mario Rabaiotti, Treasurer/kit/membership – John Davies, Club Captains, men – Gareth Ayres, John Ayres, women – Pauline Williams; general committee – John Ayres, Paul Jelley, Mandy Morris, Tony Holling; WCR Committee – Paul Rees, Ian Williams. Annual subscriptions to be increased from £5 to £10! Ian Williams sponsored the purchase of T-shirts for our invincible ladies XC team.

At a general committee meeting on 18th August there was a larger turnout of members than usual. The meeting agreed by a majority that the election of the current chairperson had been unconstitutional. It was decided to hold an EGM to discuss the matter further. A sub-committee of John Hopkins, Judith Oakley and John Davies was appointed to update the club constitution.

The EGM was held at the Briton Ferry Con Club on 17th September, where, after a somewhat heated debate, it was decided to hold a second EGM in which all officers' positions would be up for election.

The second EGM took place on 19th November at the PTH clubhouse. Bernie Henderson was voted in as chairman. Mario Rabaiotti had stood down as Secretary and was replaced by David Oak. John Davies had stood down as Treasurer/kit/membership and was replaced by the following members:- Daniel Murtagh – Treasurer, Bernie Henderson – Membership and Paul Rees – Kit.

In July, 2014 winners of the Hilly 4.8M were Helen Jones (36.22) and Gareth Ayres (28.44). The Reverse Hilly 4.8M, again organized by Darren Vaughan, was held in October and winners were Judith Oakley (34.44) and Gareth Ayres (30.19).

Meanwhile, the XC season had started again and Swansea Harriers made a determined bid to gain control of the West Glam League, leading both the male and female tables. Our ladies were not giving up easily and were lying 2nd in hot pursuit. There was still no lady's team in the Gwent League and the men's team was mid table in both XC leagues.

Clare Phillips claimed several F45 victories including Old Father Time Welsh Masters 5-mile Championship, Glynneath 5M and was also selected for Welsh Masters at the British XC Champs in Nottingham.

2014 ended with a bit of excitement when Tony Holling organized a 5K handicap race on 29th December. Joint female winners were Rosie and Cath Courts, Dennis Haynes won the men's race.

Club Championship winners were: -

Open Women – Helen Jones, Vet Women – Mandy Morris

Open Men – Gareth Ayres, Vet Men – Steve Jones

XC Women – Mandy Morris, Vet Women – Pauline Williams

XC Men – Alex Williams, Vet Men – Chris Parker

2015

In January, 2015, Darren Vaughan stepped up to organize the presentation evening at the Twelve Knights Hotel in Margam; and a good time was had by all!

There was disappointment for our ladies though. A concerted effort saw Swansea Harriers take both men's and women's titles in the West Glam XC League. After six glorious years PTH ladies had to settle for 2nd place. It was a year of seconds. The men's first team were 2nd in division 1 and the second team were 2nd in division 3 to gain promotion to division 2. Individual Overall titles were won by Helen Jones (F45), Pauline Williams (F55) and John Davies (M65). John also completed 100 consecutive Gwent League races – 20 years without missing a race.

Clare Phillips was 1st F45 in nearly every race she ran during 2015. She was also 1st lady overall in many of them, including several park runs and the 5mile Rhayader Round the Lake Race (31-22). Clare's season culminated in her selection for Welsh Masters in the XC International at Dublin in November.

The Reverse Hilly 4 was held at Tonmawr in May. Winners were: - Mandy Morris (35.26) and Steve Dinham (30.49). The PTH Half Marathon, starting and finishing at the Rhyslyn in Pontrhydyfen, was staged in August. Winners were: - Clare Phillips (1hr-31.14) and Gareth Ayres (1hr-21.10). The Hilly 4 was again from Tonmawr in October and winners were: - Mandy Morris (38.20) and Charles Walsh (33.39).

At the Welsh Masters Champs there were M40 gold medals for Charles Walsh 800m (2-25.5) and 2K Steeplechase (8-00.7). Ian Swanson M65 long jump (2.40m) and John Davies M65 javelin (29.89m). Alan Perkins and John Davies were selected for Welsh Masters at the Inter-Area Match in Solihull.

At the AGM officers elected were: - Secretary – David Oak, Chairperson/membership – Bernie Henderson, Treasurer – David Kingsland, Kit – Cath Courts.

Paul Rees oversaw another successful expedition to the Welsh Castles Relay. In the open section PTH finished 18/44 and were 22/64 overall. Charles Walsh was rather pleased to be awarded a yellow jersey as 1st M40 (57.51) on the 9.1mile 18th leg.

The second 'Have Fun and Run' initiative was a great success with over 50 people attending the first night and many more appearing over the next few weeks.

2015 saw the sad passing of two PTH servants. Ron Jones had been a field events coach specializing in the javelin and was no mean thrower himself. He spent many hours coaching and travelling the country as junior team manager. Ron passed away on 12th May at the age of 87.

Derek Tayler, father of club members Julie, Clare and Joanne, passed away on 2nd October at the age of 80. Derek was also a qualified coach specializing in the running events. He took over as PTH secretary in 1976 and eventually stood down in 1989 after making a significant contribution to the club.

Club Champs winners were: -

Open Women – Mandy Morris, Vet Women – Anna Parsons

Open Men – Gareth Ayres, Vet Men – Charles Walsh

XC Women – Mandy Morris, Vet Women – Pauline Morris

XC Men – Charles Walsh, Vet Men – Dave Cornish

2016

Our ladies returned to winning ways in the West Glam XC League in 2016. It was good teamwork that helped them become top team for the 7th time in eight years. The men remained steady in both XC leagues. Gareth Ayres continued to show great form with 2nd place in the WGXC at Aberafan Beach.

As well as helping out the XC team, Clare Phillips claimed many F45 victories and was 1st lady overall (67.25) in the Neath 10mile road race.

The club was going from strength to strength. Membership had increased to over 250. The T&F side had faded, but a new triathlon section was added thanks largely to the efforts of Darren Vaughan, Tina Ellis and Matt Anderson.

The number of coaches had also increased and sessions, very ably organized by Paul Rees, had been set up into groups of different abilities. Paul also organized another successful adventure to the Welsh Castles Relay.

Old age was taking its toll on even the seemingly ageless elders of the club. Ian Swanson was the only one fit enough to compete in the Welsh Masters Champs in 2016, winning gold medals for M65 high jump (1.10m) and 3000m (17-33.8). In August, Ian also won gold at the 5Km road race Champs. Although John Davies had retired from competing, he kept in touch with PTH and athletics in general. He qualified as a Welsh Athletics T&F

official and was regularly to be seen at PTH events with his trusty stopwatch. He was also elected treasurer of the Gwent XC League.

In May, Mandy Morris (38.23) won the women's Hilly 5 and Martin Rees (30.19) the men's race. First PTH man in 3rd place overall (33.55) was Chris Lewis.

Our club champs 1mile race was held at Western Avenue in July. Lady's winner was Claire Walters (6-09.7) and men's winner Stuart Doyle (5-27.8).

At the 5k Welsh Road Champs in August, PTH had two gold medalists. Linda Woodland was 1st F55 and Ian Swanson was 1st M65.

At the AGM in August, officers elected were: - Secretary – David Oak, Chairperson – Bernie Henderson, Treasurer – David Kingsland; Committee – Darren Vaughan, Ross Bamsey, Dennis Haines, Daniel Murtagh, Geraint Jenkins, Jane Harwood, Tina Ellis, Cath Courts, Linda Woodland, Paul Jelley; Lady's Captain – Mandy Morris, Men's Captain – Gareth Ayres.

Superbly organized by Darren Vaughan and Geraint Jenkins (and all who lent a hand), the PTH Half Marathon was held on 21st August. The male winner was Ian Harris (Swansea 1hr14.09) and first PTH was Gareth Poston (1hr-22.10). PTH made a clean sweep of the lady's race – 1st Helen Jones (1hr-39.35), 2nd Michelle Grey (1hr-41.25) and 3rd Linda Woodland (1hr-42.45).

Gareth Ayres was still in good form. His journey to Pontypool for the Ponty Plod was well worthwhile. Gareth won the race comfortably in 1hr-15.33, three minutes ahead of the second runner.

It was one small step for athletics, but one giant leap for PTH when Bernie Henderson secured the portacabin at the cricket club as our HQ. In September, 2016, Ray Cox stood down as chair of the cricket club and was replaced by Mark Jones. Mark and Ian Rees (secretary) had plans to develop the cricket club grounds. This involved demolishing the PTH portacabin which was in a dilapidated state. Mal Emerson of the Boxing Club was also keen to see PTH established in the cricket club grounds and all three were open to any suggestions from our club. In the meantime, the facilities of the cricket clubhouse were made available to PTH.

An emergency committee meeting was convened in November where the 'Building for the Future' project was approved and the plausibility of buying a specially adapted shipping container was to be investigated. The object was to raise £40,000. Liane Thomas spearheaded a brilliant social media campaign and Gareth Evans provided the technical wizardry to design the flyers.

Bernie Henderson put together a plan to raise funding for the project. For £10 each, donors could have their names, or family names, displayed on a board in the clubhouse. Local businesses etc. were invited to donate on a tiered system of bronze, silver, gold, diamond and platinum, with incentives like free memberships, depending on the size of their donation. Other fund-raising projects included a 5-a-side football tournament, a bucket collection at an Ospreys match, cake sales, curry nights and social evenings.

Significant progress had been made in 2016 and the year was brought to a close when Darren and Tanya Vaughan put on a splendid presentation evening at Blanco's in December. PTH Life Memberships were awarded to Colin Anthony, John Ayres, John Davies, Alan Furnell, Tony Holling, David Oak, Alan Perkins, Clare Phillips and Ian Swanson.

Club Champs winners were: -

Open Women – Mandy Morris, Vet Women – Linda Woodland, Super Vet Women – Carolyn Foley

Open Men – Gareth Ayres, Vet Men – Mark Hiddlestone, SuperVet Men – Bernie Henderson

XC Women – Mandy Morris, Vet Women – Helen Jones

XC Men – Dave Cornish, Vet Men – Ian Swanson

Mandy Morris, Captain & consistent winner of Club Champs

<u>2017</u>

The XC scene was quiet at the start of 2017. No wins and no team titles for PTH in the West Glam nor the Gwent League. There was one bright spot for Helen Jones who was the Individual Overall F45 winner at the end of the West Glam season.

In the quest for funding for the new clubhouse over £25,000 had been raised by the end of February, 2017. An approach was made to Tata Steel who agreed to come on board.

The club registered with the government agency, Entrust, and was able to lay hands on a £9,000 Landfill Tax. It was still not enough to cover the estimated cost of the clubhouse. At this stage, Bernie Henderson made a very generous offer. He was prepared to take out a bridging loan to cover the shortfall.

As an alternative to this offer the possibility of buying a specially adapted shipping container was resurrected. Bernie, Colin Price and Chris Williams met the NPT Planning Department who were supportive of this idea. In the meantime, the price of steel had increased and with it the price of the containers.

Joel Francis worked for Briton Ferry Construction and offered to price some options. In October, the committee accepted an offer to build the clubhouse for £39,678. The container idea was rejected in favour of a timber-framed building with a front that matched the neighbouring clubhouses. Planning permission was sought from NPT Council.

It is inevitable in the long history of this club that we will mourn the loss of loyal members. David Oak was taken ill in June and admitted to hospital where he sadly passed away on the 27th July at the relatively young age of 72. David joined PTH in 2001 and was a talented runner who had represented Wales at the 100K Celtic Plate International while a member of Neath Harriers. He was always prepared to step up to the mark when the club needed him. He took over as secretary in 2014 and stinted no effort in performing that role. On a personal note, we worked together as the PTH timekeeping team and I couldn't have wished for a better partner.

It was also a very sad day when we had to say good bye to our one and only Welsh Mile Champion from 1961, Dillwyn Robbins. Better known as Dil, he trained hard and was a keen competitor who kept meticulous records which I was fortunate enough to see thanks to his wife Christine. Dil won many track, XC and road events in his long athletic career. He sadly passed away on 29th November at 80 years of age.

The Welsh Castles Relay had become a regular fixture in the PTH calendar. It gave the members a chance to test themselves against some of the best runners in the UK. We achieved our best ever position to date in 2017 – 15/47 in the Open Category and 16/66 overall. It took great effort and organizational skills to put the team and trip together and this was supplied in no small measure by Paul Rees and Dai Parfitt.

Ian Swanson was now the only person in the club still competing at T&F. In the Welsh Masters Champs he won gold for the M65 high jump, followed by gold in the Welsh Masters 1-mile champs and went on to even greater glory with gold in the British Masters 1-mile. (Welsh and British 1-mile champs were combined in one race)

Our events team led by Darren Vaughan and Geraint Jenkins were doing a superb job. The Hilly 5 in May was won by James Hockin (West Coast Cycle,) in a new course record of 29.17. First PTH was Craig Baker (31.48). Winner of the lady's race was Mandy Morris (38.43). The half marathon, held in August, was won for the second time by Ian Harris (Swansea, 1hr13.27) and the lady's winner was Michelle Cole (3Ms, 1hr32.05). First PTH was Gareth Poston in, remarkably, exactly the same time as 2016 1hr22.10 and first PTH lady was Helen Jones (1hr39.55).

When the XC season returned in October Linda Woodland had hit a good vein of form. This resulted in her selection for Welsh Masters at the British XC International in Londonderry.

The presentation night was again a brilliant occasion thanks to the organizational skills of Darren and Tanya Vaughan. Club Championship winners were: -

Open Women – Mandy Morris, Vet Women – Linda Woodland, Super Vet Women – Ann Thomas

Open Men – Gareth Ayres, Vet Men – Mark Hiddlestone, Supervet Men – Bernie Henderson

XC Women – Many Morris, Vet Women – Linda Woodland

XC Men – Dave Cornish, Vet Men – Ian Swanson

Most Improved Woman – Allison Lloyd-Jones

Most Improved Man – Jason Jones

Multisport Women – Hazel Wheeler, Multisport Men – Timothy Williams.

A brand-new special award was created in memory of David Oak. This was presented by Gaynor Oak to Darren Vaughan whose leadership and organization of PTH events and the multisport section had been a huge asset to the club.

Linda Woodland, Welsh Masters XC International, Londonderry, 2017

<u>2018</u>

In March 2018, the XC season closed with the men's teams mid table in the West Glam XC League. The ladies couldn't quite make it to the top and were disappointed with their 2nd place in division 1. PTH had volunteered to host the last fixture at Aberafan Beach, but the race had to be called off, along with many others, because of a snowstorm a few days before.

Things were not static in the club though. A 'Couch to 5K' recruitment drive had been initiated and membership was up around the 450 mark. Along with this increase came the problem of collecting subs from so many people. The problem was solved by Liane Thomas who set up an excellent online payment system – which saved Bernie Henderson's marriage!

The coaching teams, skillfully led by Paul Rees, John Ayres, Tony Holling and Darren Vaughan (multisport), were under extra pressure because of the increased membership. Fourteen people attended the Leader in Running Fitness course and the coaching structure was altered to reflect all these changes. There were 6 groups whose abilities were based on their current best 5K time. In addition, the coaches were to be rotated on an 8-week basis in order to keep the athletes fresh and allow the coaches to develop their own skills. As a complete change, a regular track session was to be included on a separate night.

The events team led by Darren and Tanya Vaughan and Geraint Jenkins, again performed wonders doing a brilliant job of organizing some great races. The Hilly 5 in May and the half marathon in August were not only well-organised, but were affordable as well. First PTH runners in the Hilly 5 were Ben Williams (30.19) and Mandy Morris (38.50); and in the half marathon James Hockin (now a member of PTH, 1hr18.19) and Mandy Morris (1hr42.41).

Ian Swanson was the lone PTH member at the Welsh Masters T&F Champs and was rewarded with a gold medal in the 1-mile event (9-02.7).

At the AGM in August, officers elected were: - Secretary – Liane Thomas, Chairperson/membership – Bernie Henderson, Treasurer – David Kingsland; committee – Geraint Jenkins, Jane Harwood, Cath Courts, Paul Rees, Tanya Vaughan, Clare Sim, Tony Holling, Lisa Pughsley. Men's Captain – Gareth Ayres, Lady's Captain – Mandy Morris.

The clubhouse was granted planning permission in January 2018. What followed was a long period of meetings and setbacks with planning, Natural Resources Wales and Welsh Water. Bernie Henderson, Colin Price and Joel Francis worked tirelessly to keep the project

Paul Rees, leading running coach

on track. The delays actually worked to the club's advantage. The plans were revised and extra funding was sought. The final design was $3^{1/2}$ times bigger than the original portacabin.

Work began in June, 2018 and was almost finished by September. Members had their first glimpse inside the building, which had cost £42,000, on 2nd October. By the time the interior had been fitted out the cost was almost £49,000. The delays had meant that the cost was covered and Bernie's very generous offer of a bridging loan was not needed after all. So many people had been involved in the fundraising and building that it was considered a great team effort and a tremendous asset for the people of Port Talbot – the first purpose-built clubhouse that PTH had owned in the whole of their 97-year history.

Of course, while this was going on, the club was still involved in running and multisport events. The West Glam XC season started at Llanmadoc in September with some superb running from Ben Williams. He raced away from the rest of the field and was a comfortable winner in 25.45. The men were out in force in the Gwent League and by the end of the year they were top of division 3.

Thanks to the efforts of Darren and Tanya Vaughan, the presentation evening was another glittering success. Club Champs winners were: -

Open Women – Carly Thomas, Vet Women – Mandy Morris, Supervet Women – Sharon David

Open Men – Ben Williams, Vet Men – Andrew Poston, Supervet Men – Bernie Henderson

XC Women – Mandy Morris, Vet Women – Linda Woodland

XC Men – Chris Lewis, Vet Men – Dave Cornish

Multisport Women – Deb Saunders, Multisport Men – Nino Gatti

The fun event that was the 5K handicap was won by Bethan Williams and Tony Holling.

Winner of the David Oak Award for her massive contribution, not just as secretary, but in many other fields as well, was Liane Thomas.

2019

In 2019 the men's XC team were on the up. James Hockin was proving a great asset and won the Margam Park West Glam race in January. The men's first team went on to finish 2nd in division 1 and the ladies also held on to 2nd place. The men went one better in the Gwent League, topping division 3 and gaining promotion to division 2. James Hockin finished 3rd in the individual M35 table.

In May, organized by our brilliant events team Darren and Tanya Vaughan and Geraint Jenkins plus their dozens of helpers, the Hilly 5 was again a great success. Leading PTH runners were James Hockin (2nd, 26.49) and Mandy Morris (4th, 39.38). The team also put on another very successful Tata Steelman Triathlon and Aquathlon series at Aberafan Beach. Cathryn Williams was Overall Individual Ladies Winner of the aquathlon events.

Ian Swanson was the only PTH left standing at the Welsh Masters Champs. He leaped to a M65 gold medal in the long jump (2.28m).

In August our super events team put on the PTH Half Marathon at Glyncorrwg. The race was well-received and there were many complimentary remarks on Facebook. Top runners for PTH were Jenny Blackmore (4th, 1hr 43.33) and James Hockin (3rd, 1hr 17.23).

The new clubhouse had been finished and in use for part of 2019. It was time for a grand official opening which took place on 17th August. Guest of Honour was Nia Singleton of Tata Steel who cut the tape and declared the new building open to start a new era in the history of PTH.

In 2018, Bernie Henderson and Caryn Furlow attended a meeting organized by Sport Wales. The dangers of PTH not being a Charitable Incorporated Organization were explained. This was brought back to the committee who agreed that this was a necessary change. At the 2019 AGM the members approved also and an application form was submitted to the Charity Commission. The application required a constitution to be submitted and this necessitated stripping out most of the sporting items from the PTH constitution. This process took several months and was not completed in 2019.

Officers elected at the AGM were: - Secretary – Lianne Thomas with Clare Sim, Chairperson/membership – Bernie Henderson, Treasurer – David Kingsland; Committee – Jane Harwood, Paul Rees, Tanya Vaughan, Amy Hines, Martyn Hines, Lisa Clement-Jones; Men's Captain – Rob Kestin, Lady's Captain – Mandy Morris. Gareth Ayres had stood down after seven years of sterling service as Club Captain.

On the multisport side there were international honours for four club members. David Morgan, Craig Dummer and Carl Singleton represented GB M40 at the Long-Distance European Triathlon in Amsterdam. Paul Bennett represented GB M60 at the World Aquathlon Champs in Pontevedra, Spain.

The XC season returned in the autumn of 2019 with all teams consolidating their positions in both leagues. There were some good individual performances and the following PTH members were selected for West Wales at the Inter-Area Champs in Brecon – Rob Kestin, Charles Walsh, Chris Lewis, Mark Hiddlestone, Martin Hines, Sam Figgures, Mandy Morris, Nichola Wilcox, Julia Jones, Cathryn Williams, Carolyn Williams, Lisa Clement-Jones, Linzi Margetson, Sian Mahoney and Jill Peacock. James Hockin went one better and represented Wales M35 at the British XC International in Liverpool, finishing a respectable 20th in his age group.

Rob Kestin was in fine form over the ultra-distances in 2019. Included in his victories were trail half and full marathons and several pbs over various distances. His best performance came in the Pembrokeshire 100 miles which he won in 24hr 36.10 beating the 2nd runner by over two hours. And just to show he had a turn of speed he won the PTH club champs 1-mile race as well!

Clare Phillips had been having a problem with her hip for some time and throughout 2017 couldn't run while she was waiting for a hip replacement. The operation eventually took place in April 2018 when Clare had a new state of the art metal hip. She started running a few months later and ran the Swansea park run in December in the amazing time of 24-31. During 2019 Clare raced regularly, winning several of the park runs, while her times gradually improved to a best of 21-31, a remarkable recovery.

Although not fit enough to compete, John Davies was still active with Welsh Masters as a track judge and timekeeper. At their AGM in November, he was presented with the Dave Williams Commemorative Trophy for his services to WMAA – the only person to be awarded this trophy twice.

So, the end of year celebrations came around once more with a banquet at Blanco's laid on by Darren and Tanya Vaughan. Club Champs winners were: -

Open Women – Mandy Morris, Vet Women – Helen Jones, Supervet Women – Carolyn Foley

Open Men – Craig Foley, Vet Men – Andrew Poston, Supervet Men – Bernie Henderson

XC Women – Mandy Morris, Vet Women – Nichola Wilcox

XC Men – Ian Swanson, Vet Men – Chris Lewis

Multisport Women – Cathryn Williams/Ffion Davies (tied), Multisport Men – Nino Gatti.

David Oak Award – Geraint Jenkins, for his unstinting work in all of the PTH events.

Darren Vaughan – Leading Triathlon Coach and Volunteer of the Year, 2020

2020s

2020

Well, what a year that was! It started off with a bang at the NPT Physical Activity and Sports Service Awards at a packed Princess Royal Theatre on 17th January. PTH were worthy winners of the Senior Club Team of the Year award. The Volunteer of the Year award deservedly went to Darren Vaughan. It was no surprise to PTH members who were all proud and delighted for Darren. The amount of work he had put into the club was phenomenal and the award was thoroughly deserved.

The year continued with XC in full swing. Nino Gatti, Robert Kestin, Gareth Ayres and James Hockin were all in fine form and James won the WGXC Tata Lake race (29.38). For the ladies Mandy Morris, Pauline Williams, Helen Jones, Clare Phillips, Nichola Wilcox and Cathryn Williams were well to the fore.

There was bad news for PTH in March, though, when Mandy and Pauline transferred to Neath Harriers, mainly because the interest in XC at PTH had waned. There was further bad news in June when Linda Woodland and Nichola Wilcox also left for Neath.

News came through early in the year about some Covid virus spreading rapidly in China. No one in the UK was worried about it – until the dratted thing broke out here, and our world was turned upside down! But - it didn't stop Mandy Morris and Nichola Wilcox from running for West Wales in the Inter-Counties at Loughborough in early March. Soon after, all sports were cancelled.

The West Glam XC League was reduced to four races instead of the usual five. The final tables showed a healthy position for all three PTH teams who were lying 2nd in their respective divisions. Nichola Wilcox was F40 individual champion and Helen Jones F50 champion. Clare Phillips picked up in 2020 where she left off in 2019. She was 1st F50 in both the Ponty Reverse 10M (71-41) and the WGXC round the lake race (39-19). Clare also won the Swansea park run improving her best time to a brilliant 20-59.

The running year was over virtually before it had started; but wait a minute, did someone mention virtual running? Martin Hines organized a series of virtual races where runners ran a socially distanced time trial on any course, but over a specific distance. The results were compiled by Lianne Thomas from Strava etc. and a race result was produced as well as an age-graded result to make it fairer for the elderly members! The 'winners' were: -

1 mile – Cathryn Williams, 6-15; Craig Foley, 4-50

1 mile age graded – Sharon David, 5-58; Craig Foley, 4-49

2 mile – Magda ap Robert, 14-44; Craig Foley, 10-31

2 mile age graded – Magda ap Robert, 14-20; Mark Hiddlestone, 10-19

3 mile – Cathryn Williams, 21-27; Craig Foley, 15-37

3 mile age graded – Sharon David; Craig Foley, 15-34

4 mile – Cathryn Williams, 28-07; Craig Foley, 21-33

4 mile age graded – Sharon David, 27-10; Craig Foley, 21-31

Bernie Henderson, PTH Chairman

The new club constitution was ready in June and the application was sent to the Charity Commission. A few items had still to be clarified, but on 21st July PTH was accepted officially as a Charitable Incorporated Organisation. One of the requirements was that there be twelve Trustees and four of them had to stand down or stand for re-election at every AGM. The first list of Trustees was comprised of the officers and committee of the club – Bernie Henderson, Lianne Thomas, David Kingsland, Clare Sim, Paul Rees, Jane Harwood, Amy Hines, Martin Hines, Helen Griffiths, Robert Kestin, Katy Martin, Tanya Vaughan.

As the Covid virus took hold, training had to be modified to accommodate social distancing and was cancelled completely during a couple of total lockdowns. The coaches, led by Paul Rees and Bernie Henderson, did a great job of reorganizing the training schedules and areas to accommodate the social distancing. In December, the Pfizer vaccine was given approval for use by the MHRA regulatory body. There was light at the end of the Covid tunnel.

In the meantime, PTH was involved in several more virtual events. The 15hour CardiffGait Relay was held in June with two PTH teams taking part. The 'A' team finished 27th and the 'B' team 32nd out of 58 clubs.

The PTH virtual Hilly 5 was held in August. 'Winners' were Andrew Poston (31-56) and Rebekah Thomas (40-04).

Mark Hiddlestone took part in all three of the Swansea Bay Virtual 5K Series and did incredibly well. He won the first race (19-47), was 3rd in the second race (22-42) and 2nd in the final race (19-32). Mark also won the silver medal for 2nd place individual overall.

The virtual London Marathon was held on the 4th October. There were a dozen or so members out including Chairperson Bernie Henderson who recorded a more than useful 3hrs 35.01. Best times of the day were Ben Phillips (3hrs 08.31) and Teresa Jefferies-Callaghan (5hrs 01.00).

On 11th October PTH took part in another 15hour virtual relay which turned out to be extremely successful. Both 'A' and 'B' teams took 1st place in the event clocking 133.7 and 101.56 miles respectively.

This success was soon to be overshadowed by a tragic event later in the month. Garry Vaughan was taken ill and rushed into hospital where, after an emergency operation, he sadly passed away on 26th October. Garry was an accomplished triathlete and well-respected coach. He was only 41 and married with two young children. He was respected and loved by everyone who knew him and as a testament to his popularity, hundreds of mourners lined the road near the Twelve Knights, clapping as his funeral cortege slowly passed.

After this extremely sad and traumatic loss it was difficult to return to athletics. The Richard Burton 10K was scheduled for 1st November and many members had trained specifically for it. The result was that the race was dedicated to the memory of Garry Vaughan. 146 members took part and the leading PTH runners were Craig Foley (33-41) and Cathryn Williams (42-10). Along with the 10k there was a mini-miler fun run. It was a case of little chips off the old block for leading runners Ryan Hiddlestone (8-32) and Molly Richards (10-19).

The next challenge came on 28/29th November with the Reason2Run Relay. Each athlete ran for 30 minutes making it 48 runners over 24 hours who totalled 194.79 miles for 1st place and comfortably ahead of 2nd team R4A who recorded 188.19 miles.

The AGM was delayed by Covid until 30th November and had to take place via Zoom. There were no nominations for officers and committee because the new CIO status required the Trustees to make these appointments. The rules also stated that four Trustees had to stand down or stand for re-election at the AGM. Bernie Henderson, Paul Rees and Helen Griffiths were re-elected. Tanya Vaughan stood down and was replaced by Craig Williams. There were three nominations for lady's captain. Jane Harwood was elected as captain and Cathryn Williams vice-captain. Robert Kestin was returned unopposed as the worthy men's captain. There were four new Life Members elected, all of them having represented GB at World or European triathlon or aquathlon. PTH is very honoured to have them as members – David Morgan, Carl Singleton, Craig Dummer and Paul Bennett. Longtime coach, chairman and president, Peter David was promoted to Honorary Life President.

Another of the famous O'Brien family sadly passed away in 2020. Aneurin O'Brien was a talented young runner of great potential. In 1958, he was 2nd in the YMCA Junior XC Champs and went on to represent Wales at the British YMCA XC Champs. Aneurin retired from competition at an early age and remained a respected member of the community. He was a devoted father and grandfather when he passed away at the age of 79 on 3rd December.

On a personal note, I've always referred to myself by name rather than in the first person because I didn't want this book to sound like an autobiography. I'm making an exception here though, because I was completely overwhelmed when Bernie asked me if I'd like to be President of PTH. I have to say that I was delighted to accept such a great honour and I'm very pleased and very proud to be the President of the best athletic/multisport club in Wales. 2020 wasn't such a bad year for me after all!

2021

So, we have arrived at last at the Centennial Year of Port Talbot Harriers. As I write this, we are still locked down and in the grip of the Covid 19 pandemic. To add to the problems, the virus has mutated and there are several strains striving for dominance.

PTH still survives, however, and the trustees have worked hard to ensure that the members are kept involved. There have been several on-line quiz events superbly organized by Craig Williams. David Morgan and Darren Vaughan have done a brilliant job on the Zwift meetings for the multisport members. Rob Kestin, Chris John and Jane Harwood put their clever heads together to produce a one/month series of virtual events for the runner's club championship.

The first of the club champs was a one-mile virtual run. Any number of attempts could be made during January, but only the best time would count. There was a great response to this challenge and the best times recorded were: -

Men – Craig Foley 4-44.9; Vet Men – Dave Kingsland 5-07.3; Supervet Men – Brian Lewis 6-19.0

Women – Cathryn Williams 6-05.0; Vet Women – Sian Wyndham 7-19.0; Supervet Women – Sharon David 7-45.0

The lock-down continued through February. The Covid cases started dropping off and the vaccination roll-out continued at a rapid pace. The UK had the highest vaccination rate in the world.

The trustees continued to meet via Zoom online and Craig Williams organized a very enjoyable virtual quiz for the members.

Still no club training sessions, but a large number of PTH members completed the virtual club championship tester over 5 miles. The best times recorded were: -

Men – Craig Foley 26-54; Vet Men – David Kingsland 29-19; Supervet – Paul Jelley 35-42
Women – Debby Saunders 34-13; Vet Women – Jenny Blackmore 37-16; Supervet Women – Sharon David 43-22.

The Ras Dewi Sant 40-mile Ultra Marathon made a welcome return on March 27th after being cancelled in 2020. It was even more welcome for our club captain, Robert Kestin. Rob took the undulating course in his stride and ran superbly to win in a terrific time of 6hrs-50-27, holding off a strong challenge from 2nd placed Sean Rice.

There was no virtual race in the club champs. This time the challenge was to complete at least 50 miles in the month of March. There was a more than enthusiastic response to this task. Top of the table was Richard Davies who clocked 309.8 miles and the ladies mileage leader was Debby Saunders with 199 miles.

The virtual challenge for April/May was the Tonmawr Hilly 5. Most people chose to run the actual course – which certainly lives up to its name! The best times recorded in each age category were: -

Men – Craig Foley, 28-35; Vet Men – Andrew Poston, 32-30; Supervet Men – Brian Lewis, 41-13
Women – Debby Saunders, 36-41; vet Women – Lesley Mainwaring, 41-32; Supervet Women – Sharon David, 49.08.

Looking for a new challenge, Tony Holling had taken up triathlon in his old age. There is a saying *'You can't teach an old dog new tricks'*. In Tony's case this is definitely not true. He competed in the Cotswold Olympic Triathlon in May and won the M60 category in a time of 3hrs 53-36 in 85th place overall out of 245 entries.

PTH took part in the Builth & District 15-hour Virtual Relay on 13th June. Each runner was required to run for 30 minutes at a specific time on a course of their choice. There were some excellent runs from Nino Gatti (5.15 miles) and David Kingsland (5.08 miles) For the ladies, Sarah Howard (4.18 miles) and Zoe Davies (4.05 miles) led the way. PTH finished 3rd overall with a cumulative total of 115.71 miles.

The virtual club championship continued through the summer with hardly any relaxation of the Covid regulations. Numbers competing were down, but there were some good performances. Best times for the Margam Mountain Run were recorded by Craig Foley (58.28) and Debby Saunders (1hr 13-57).

The Smallwood Road Challenge was a hill too far for most members. In fact, the ladies were twice as brave as the men – 22 ladies took part to 11 men. Best times were Adrian Weaver (13.03) and Debby Saunders (14.56).

It is now 15th September, 2021 as I write. I'm bringing this account to a close so that the book will be available for the Centenary celebrations on 15th October. There have been many ups and downs for PTH over the past century. We have seen super individual performances, Welsh Championships, British honours and very many team titles. It took Arthur Williams more than 50 years to realise his ambition of a running track at Western Avenue. He would have been hugely disappointed that his dream was shattered by unthinking planners when the track was demolished to make way for the new Bae Baglan School. Couldn't it have been retained as part of the sporting facilities for the new school? From 1961 onwards PTH had a rather nomadic existence with no place they could call their own. Schools, rugby clubs, leisure centres and car parks were all utilized until, finally, a grand plan for a clubhouse was formed. Today, we find PTH firmly established in our own clubhouse thanks to the sterling efforts of the committee and members. With numbers increasing and a thriving multisport section, the next 100 years holds great promise. I wish the club, committee and members all good fortune for the next 100 years.

(ps – All we need now is a track and field team to reflect the glory of the early years!)

Port Talbot Harriers 100

John Davies

APPENDIX – WELSH CHAMPIONS

WAAA CHAMPIONS – SENIOR MEN

100 yards	Will Owen	1923	10.2
	Will Owen	1924	10.6
	Harry Anderson	1929	10.2

440 yards	Roy Williams	1938	51.4
	John Collins	1952	51.7

1 mile	Dillwyn Robbins	1961	4-21.6

Pole Vault	Cyril Evans	1937	2.74m
	Cyril Evans	1938	3.11m
	G. H. Thorne	1947	2.72m
	Cyril Evans	1948	3.20m

Javelin	Jim Boyle	1967	57.38m

WAAA CHAMPIONS - U20 MEN

100 yards	Keith Maddocks	1944	10.8

440 yards	Roy Williams	1936	55.0

880 yards	Brinley Quick	1935	2-15.0

1 Mile	Lyn Griffiths	1938	4-52.0

120 Yards Hurdles Keith Davitte 1955 16.4

Keith Davitte 1956 16.5

WAAA CHAMPIONS - U17 BOYS

200m Shaun Whelan 1978 24.4

Andrew Millard 1984 24.9

800m Michael Cole 1973 2-02.9

Shaun Whelan 1979 1-56.26

100 yards Hurdles Keith Davitte 1953 15.2

Terry Schneider 1961 14.5

Terry Schneider 1962 14.1

Shot Put Andrew Millard 1986 12.85m

Javelin Graham Robinson 1963 52.52m

Graham Robinson 1964 56.72m

WAAA CHAMPIONS - U15 BOYS

80 yards Hurdles Terry Schneider 1952 10.9

800m Michael Cole 1972 2-06.4

1500m Andrew Millard 1979 4-24.2

High Jump Keith Davitte 1952 1.52m

WAAA CHAMPIONS – SENIOR WOMEN

There were no championships for women in 1937, but Nellie Denner recorded the fastest times in Wales for 100yards – 11.9 and 220yards – 28.6

80m Hurdles   Gaynor Blackwell   1971   16.0

5Km
	Kath Williams	1980	17-45.2
	Louise Copp	1982	17-45.0
	Liz Williams	1983	18-18.4
	Clare Phillips	2010 (road)	18-57

WAAA CHAMPIONS – U20 WOMEN

200m   Sian Morris   1983   24.6

3Km   Emily Crowley   2000   11-07.38

Javelin   Julie Tayler   1983   34.76m

WAAA CHAMPIONS – U17 GIRLS

100m   Sian Morris   1980   12.5

200m   Sian Morris   1980   25.9

400m   Sian Morris   1981   59.0

880 Yards   Shirley Ellis   1967   2-38.3

800m   Louise Copp   1979   2-20.2
           Debbie Crowley   1983   2-20.6

1500m   Lisa Carthew   1986   4-52.8

80m Hurdles   Gaynor Blackwell   1969   12.7
              Gaynor Blackwell   1970   12.8

WAAA CHAMPIONS – U15 GIRLS

800m   Louise Copp   1978   2-24.7
        Debbie Crowley   1981   2-25.5

1500m   Kath Williams   1978   4-52.2
        Debbie Crowley   1981   4-54.6
        Lisa Carthew   1985   4-54.1

High Jump   Pam Walker   1977   1.55m
            Pam Walker   1978   1.58m
Long Jump   Paula Thomas 1978   5.30m

Javelin   Julie Tayler   1978   28.72
          Julie Tayler   1979   38.34

WAAA CHAMPIONS – U13 GIRLS

100m   Ceri Stephens   1989   13.5
200m   Ceri Stephens   1989   27.5
800m   Lisa Carthew   1983   2-32.8
1500m   Julie Crowley   1983   5-11.1
Javelin   Julie Tayler 1977   22.82m

WAAA CROSS COUNTRY CHAMPIONS – MEN

7 mile XC Champion   Jim O'Brien   1961

WAAA XC CHAMPIONS – U20

Brynley Quick   1937

Tom Winslade   1938   (PTYMCA Harriers team winners in 1938)

Jim Davies   1948

John Nash   1950

WAAA XC CHAMPIONS – U17

Brynley Quick   1935

WAAA XC CHAMPIONS – NOVICE

D. J. P. Richards   1922

(PTYMCA Harriers team winners in 1937)

WAAA CROSS COUNTRY CHAMPIONS – WOMEN

WAAA XC CHAMPIONS – U17 GIRLS

Katrina Blackwell   1970

Kath Williams   1980

Kath Williams   1981

WAAA XC CHAMPIONS – U15 GIRLS

Katrina Blackwell   1969

Debbie Crowley   1981

Debbie Crowley   1982

Julie Crowley   1986

WAAA XC CHAMPIONS – U13 GIRLS

Kath Williams   1977

Debbie Crowley   1980

Julie Crowley   1984

(U20 women won the team championship in 1981)

WAAA ROAD RELAY CHAMPIONS

U15 GIRLS

1978 – Louise Copp, Clare Paisley, Liz Williams, Kath Williams

1980 – Debbie Brambley, Bev Morgan, Debbie Crowley, Cath Corish,

1981 – Debbie Brambley, Debbie Crowley, Ceri Brambley, Bev Morgan

U13 GIRLS

1979 – Clare Phillips, Cath Corish, Susan James, Debbie Crowley

WAAA MARATHON CHAMPIONS – MEN

1937 – Isaac O'Brien 3 hrs 03-16

1938 – Isaac O'Brien 2 hrs 58-23

1939 – Isaac O'Brien 2 hrs 45-00

WAAA ULTRA- MARATHON (40 miles)

1997 – Anthony Holling 4 hrs 48-23

WELSH SCHOOLS CHAMPIONS – BOYS

Senior 80 yards Hurdles	Keith Davitte	1956	16.4
Junior 75 Yards Hurdles	Terry Schneider	1960	10.9
Middle 400m	Jeff Griffiths	1973	52.2
	Jeff Griffiths	1974	52.0

Junior 800m	Michael Cole	1972	2-11.0
	Shaun Whelan	1978	2-06.2
Middle 800m	Shaun Whelan	1979	1-58.7
Senior pole vault	Les Keen	1972	3.30m

WELSH SCHOOLS CHAMPIONS – GIRLS

Senior 200m	Sian Morris	1983	25.3
Middle 400m	Sian Morris	1981	57.7
Junior 800m	Louise Copp	1978	2-23.8
	Julie Crowley	1985	2-22.5
Middle 800m	Katrina Blackwell	1970	2-23.3
	Louise Copp	1979	2-21.7
	Julie Crowley	1986	2-19.8
	Julie Crowley	1987	2-20.2
Junior 1500m	Cath Corish	1980	4-58.1
	Debbie Crowley	1981	4-53.1
	Laura Carthew	1987	4-48.5
Middle 1500m	Kath Williams	1979	4-47.9
	Debbie Crowley	1982	4-50.7
Junior 3Km	Kath Williams	1980	10-21.5
Middle 3Km	Lisa Carthew	1987	10-35.8
Senior 3Km	Beverly Morgan	1985	10-50.9
Middle 80m Hurdles	Gaynor Blackwell	1969	11.9

	Gaynor Blackwell	1970	11.6
Senior 100m Hurdles	Gaynor Blackwell	1971	16.5
Senior Long Jump	Gaynor Blackwell	1971	5.14m
Junior Javelin	Julie Tayler	1977	36.10m
Junior High Jump	Pamela Walker	1977	1.49m
	Pamela Walker	1978	1.60m
Middle High Jump	Pamela Walker	1979	1.59m

WELSH SCHOOLS INTER-COUNTIES CROSS COUNTRY CHAMPIONS

Junior – 1978 – Kath Williams

     1980 – Debbie Crowley

     1981 – Debbie Crowley

     1985 – Lisa Carthew

Middle – 1982 – Debbie Crowley

     1986 – Julie Crowley

Senior – 1981 – Kath Williams

     1985 – Beverly Morgan

BRITISH SCHOOLS CROSS COUNTRY INTERNATIONAL CHAMPIONS

Junior – 1980- Debbie Crowley

     1981 – Debbie Crowley

     1985 – Lisa Carthew

Intermediate – 1979 – Kath Williams

     1980 – Kath Williams

PTH – WELSH TRACK & FIELD LEAGUE WINNERS

MEN'S 1978 – Division 3;   1991 – Division 5

WOMEN'S   1980 – Division 2;   1983 – Division 3

COMBINED WOMEN & MEN   2000 – Division 3

WELSH YMCA CHAMPION CLUB

1922,1923,1925,1926,1928,1929, 1947, 1948, 1951

AAA UK CHAMPIONS

U17 Girls 60m hurdles – Gaynor Blackwell, 1970

U15 Girls javelin – Julie Tayler, 1979

British Masters Indoor T&F Champions – Men

M75

2010 – Len Tew 800m 2-56.45; 1500m 6-00.10

British Masters Outdoor T&F Champions- Men

M75

2010 – Len Tew 400m 74.20; 800m 3-26.18; 1500m 6-07.68

British Masters 1-Mile Champion

M65

2017 – Ian Swanson

WELSH MASTERS CHAMPIONS

2002 – WMAA T+F Champion Club PTH

M40

1989 – John Davies   Javelin 39.20m

1991 – John Davies   Javelin 39.78m; 100m 13.4

1992 – Ian Swanson   Long Jump 3.86m

      John Davies   Javelin 35.28m; 400mH 73.8; Triple Jump 8.75m

1993 – John Davies   Javelin 34.22m

      Ian Swanson   400mH 84.7; High Jump 1.30m

      Alan Perkins   1500m 4-44.1

2008 – Vince Lewis   400m 55.6

2010 – Vince Lewis   400m

2014 - Charles Walsh   100m 13.1; 800m 2-19.3; 1500m 4-59.1

2015 – Charles Walsh   800m 2-25.5; 2K Steeplechase 8-00.7

M45

1997 – John Davies   100m 13.98; 200m 28.59

1998 – John Davies   Javelin 36.39m; 800m 2-33.5; 1500m 5-11.5

2014 – Vince Lewis   400m 59.7

F45

2014 – Clare Phillips   5-mile road 32-02

M50

1991 – Geoff Pugh   800m; Triple Jump

1993 – Geoff Pugh   800m 2-19.8; 1500m 4-54.9

1999 - John Davies   Javelin 34.63m; 100m 14.71; 200m 29.40

2000 – John Davies   Javelin 35.84m; Discus 23.72m

      Ian Swanson   High Jump 1.25m

2001 – Alan Perkins   1500m 5-00.6

      Ian Swanson   High Jump 1.25m, Triple Jump 7.26m

2002 – John Davies   Javelin 37.89m

2003 – John Davies   Javelin 38.60m; Hammer 23.02m

      Ian Swanson   High Jump 1.20m

2006 – Tony Holling   5K 21-46.0;   40mile   5hrs-36.05

2007 – Tony Holling   40mile   5hrs-29.57

M55

1993 – Jim O'Brien   10K 36-17.2; 5K 17-52.7

2004 – John Davies   Javelin 38.04m; 800m 2-49.5; 1500m 5-59.0

2005 – John Davies   Javelin 35.88m; Hammer 24.78m; Shot 7.35m; Discus 25.06m

2006 – John Davies   Javelin 34.99m; Hammer 24.18m; Discus 26.15m

2007 – Alan Perkins   Marathon 3hrs-42-12

        John Davies   Javelin 36.12m

2008 – Alan Perkins   Marathon 3hrs-51

        John Davies   Javelin 25.90m; Hammer 25.37m; Discus 25.54m

F55

2016 – Linda Woodland   5Km Road

M60

2009 – John Davies   Javelin 38.44m; Hammer 26.21m; Discus 28.98m; Shot 7.41m;
                      800m 2-59.4; 1500m 6-01.7

2010 – John Davies   Javelin 35.88m; Hammer 25.68m; Discus 31.14m; Shot 7.75m

        Ian Swanson High Jump; Triple Jump; Long Jump; 5K (road) 28.00

2011 – John Davies   Javelin 32.00m; Hammer 26.07m; Discus 28.36m; Shot 6.75m

        Ian Swanson   High Jump   1.10m

2012 – John Davies   Javelin 30.96m

2013 – John Davies   Javelin 29.45m; Hammer 22.84m; Discus 22.84m; 1500m 7-00.17

2014 – Ian Swanson   High Jump 1.15m

M65

2014 – John Davies   Javelin 28.72m; 1500m 6-33.7

2015 – John Davies   Javelin 29.89m

        Ian Swanson   Long Jump 2.04m

2016 – Ian Swanson   High Jump 1.10m; 3Km 17-33.8; 5Km Road

2017 – Ian Swanson   High Jump 1.10m, 1-mile

2018 – Ian Swanson   1-mile 9-02.7

2019 – Ian Swanson   Long Jump 2.28m

<u>M75</u>

2010 – Len Tew   800m 2-59.7

Who am I?

<u>John Davies</u> – Born into a mining family in Cwmafan, Port Talbot, 02/09/1948. Attended Glanafan Grammar School and worked for over 30 years as a chemist at BP Chemicals, Baglan Bay. Happily married to Adrianne since 1971. One son, Ian, happily married to Tina and they have three children Freya, Ayla and Osian.

Association with PTH began in 1967 when workmate and PTH Chairman, Derek Moss, persuaded me to join. Other sports and family commitments meant a break until 1983 when I rejoined. Since then, roles undertaken at PTH have been: - co-founder, with Kevin Corcoran, and organizer of club champs; author of Paperchase newsletter; press officer; photographer; Gwent XC men's team manager; race organizer; Master's T&F team manager; Kit secretary; membership secretary; minutes secretary; presentation night organizer; treasurer; timekeeper; chairman.

Club veteran Champion; Welsh Masters champion in many T&F events; ranked 1st in Welsh javelin and 4th in UK javelin M55; president Welsh Masters 2000-2004; treasurer Gwent XC League 2016-2020. Currently - qualified Welsh Athletics T&F judge, timekeeper, endurance official, race referee and adjudicator; life member and president of PTH.

Printed in Great Britain
by Amazon